GOD *of the* COMEBACK

Dr. Michael Maiden

TRILOGY PUBLISHING
Tustin, CA

First originally published by Trilogy Publishing 2018

ISBN 978-1-64088-075-7 (Paperback)
ISBN 978-1-64088-076-4 (Digital)

Printed in the United States of America

DEDICATION

This book is dedicated to my amazing wife, Mary, and our four children: Melody, Matthew, Timothy, and Christina. I am so humbled and eternally grateful for the gifts God has given me in my family. All of our children have such beautiful hearts so many amazing abilities. But my children and I know that the real hero in our beloved family is their mother, my wife, the beautiful Mary.

WHAT OTHERS ARE SAYING...

"I highly recommend this book to be read by Preachers, Teachers, and Disciples. It is the right time.

"I hope that reading this will inspire each of us to become more transparent in sharing what God's grace has enabled us to become. Obedience, forgiveness, loving our enemies, are just words until the Holy Spirit puts a demand on us personally to act. The pain of rejection, betrayal, loss, disappointment and physical pain all tend toward self pity and anger which we justify by declaring the unfairness of it.

"Dr. Maiden does not give us cliches nor quick fixes, but clearly and transparently shows the struggle of climbing out of depression hour by hour, until total victory was his and personal pain gone, family and church revived, and double portion blessed all.

"In closing he exposes the reason God allows these situations to afflict his people by reminding us of the One 'who comforts us in all our tribulation, that we may be able to comfort those who are in any trouble, with the comfort with which we ourselves are comforted by God.' (2 Cor. 1:4)"

Dr. Iverna M. Tompkins
Iverna Tompkins Ministries
Scottsdale, Az

"You are about to be profoundly challenged and inspired through this remarkable book. Michael Maiden's story is both heart-wrenching and unusually encouraging.

"We hear of injustices happening all around us, but rarely do we see one that is so blatant and destructive. Even more rare is the redemptive response that the Maidens' gave to their critics and betrayers. They could have run, just to avoid the unjust pressure coming their way. No one would have blamed them. Instead they stayed in the city they were called to, believing God would have the last say.

"And He did. The *God of the Comeback* is the testimony of God's faithfulness that *prophesies* that His desire is to do the same for every one of us. Please read this in hope for anything that seems to be beyond hope. And let's watch together as the *God of the Comeback* once again turns tragedy into triumph!"

Bill Johnson
Bethel Church – Redding, CA
Author – *God is Good*

"Someone once said: 'God can't use a person until He first hurts them.' This hasn't always set well with my faith position but I think Mike Maiden, our modern day Job provides us a living illustration.

"To say that the Maidens took a trip to hell and back would be an understatement. They were given a one way ticket and lived in hell for years.

"God of the Comeback brought me to tears but more than that, brought me closer to answering this question; If God is so good, then why all the pain and suffering in the world? Finally, a man of faith, with the right attitude, grants us a spiritual explanation for pain and suffering.

"I could not put the book down. I found myself rejoicing and weeping with the Maidens. *God of The Comeback* is now a required reading for all our executives and pastors.

"Thanks, Dr Maiden or shall I say, Thanks, Dr Job."

Mike D. Robertson
Lead Pastor, Visalia First
Visalia, California

"The first time I sat with Michael and heard the story of what God had done in his life my heart was stirred. What an incredible gift to be able to see God at work in such a profound way in our lives.

"*God of the Comeback* is more than just a book, it is a prophetic declaration for your life. Every person should read this book to increase their faith and gain a deeper revelation of the grace and goodness of God."

Banning Liebscher
Jesus Culture Founder and Pastor
Author of *Rooted: The Hidden Places Where God Develops Us*

"This book is a testament to the awesome power, goodness and grace of God. If you find yourself depressed and broken or even on top of the world, let God of the Comeback strengthen your resolve in this truth: While you may be 'struck down' in this life, you are far from destroyed. Dr. Maiden's personal journey, from the depths of sorrow and betrayal to the fullness of restoration, reminds us all that God will indeed finish the work he started."

Rev. Samuel Rodriguez
President, National Hispanic Christian Leadership Conference
Nominated by TIME Magazine as one of the top 100 influential leaders in America.

"Everyone in life experiences failures or setbacks. In *God of the Comeback,* written by Dr. Michael Maiden, you will read one of the most incredible stories of a man and his family getting up from having lost everything and coming back better than ever! If you or someone you love finds them self in that place, I fully recommend you pick up this book and read it! The principles taught by Dr. Maiden have the potential to bring a powerful comeback for you!"

Jim Bolin
Founding Pastor, Trinity Chapel
Life Coach, Author - *The Rope of Hope*

"Dr. Michael Maiden willingness to bare all about his experience with betrayal, deception, loss, identity and depression will bring help and healing to many souls. Everyone at some point in their life will need to read this book. I want to thank him for reminding us that even when we feel that all is lost, and everything is gone, God's heart will always beat relentlessly with love towards us. This is a wonderful book!"

James Haizlip
Founder and Senior Pastor, The
Sanctuary, Orange County, CA

FOREWORD

" I count Dr. Michael Maiden one of my dearest friends and comrades in ministry. His fatherly heart and prophetic insight has changed lives globally, including mine. I have known him for quite a long time. His journey from being one of the leading pastors in the Scottsdale, Arizona during the height of the Charismatic Movement, to the pain of having someone on staff embezzle tens of millions of dollars, and the loss of everything from church, to home, to reputation, to a personal sense of well-being was a painful and dark season to endure.

"I remember a profound conversation with Dr. Lawrence Kennedy, about how amazing it was that Dr. Michael (who was totally innocent) chose to stay in the area (when most others would have left), in the midst of false accusations, allegations, smear campaigns and federal investigations, and yet, he and his wife did not leave out of a conviction that God was going to do something fresh and new.

"Today, Church for the Nations, is one of the leading multi-campus expressions of the Body of Christ in the greater Phoenix, Arizona region. It is also an apostolic center for the dissemination of the Gospel globally. It thrives and pulses with the life-giving power and demonstration of the Spirit, with a fresh and vital message of the Crucified, Resurrected, and Ascended Christ and His amazing grace.

"When the Scripture speaks of God giving us beauty for ashes, it is a genuine revelation of both the love of God the Father as revealed through the work of Christ at the Cross by the power of the Spirit to turn our sufferings into something glorious that rises above the ashes to a place of power and authority that is unquestionable. To know Dr. Maiden, and to be in what God has built through him in the greater Phoenix area, is to experience the fruit of a lengthy season of testing, trial, persecution, and suffering, that ultimately yielded to a resurrection out from the ashes of former sufferings into a glorious expression of the goodness and the compassion of God. You cannot listen to any one of Dr. Maiden's messages or read any one of his writings, and not be deeply stirred and moved by his profound insights into the Person of Jesus, the love of the Father, and the indwelling of the Holy Spirit.

"In *God Of The Comeback*, you are going to learn the secrets of how to anticipate the goodness of God when you would be tempted to despair that you would see that goodness in the land of the living because of the trials and setbacks you may be facing. Dr. Maiden is quite transparent and vulnerable in these pages, in order that out of what God opened up in him through his tests and trials, you might benefit and receive from. He admits to blind spots (that we all have by the way), and in so doing, invites us into the windows of his own soul and the journey got brought him through to get him to where he is.

"I am mindful of the old charismatic chorus, 'Look what the Lord has done.' Walk into Church for the Nations today, and you would want to sing that song: hear the worship, experience the power and presence of the Risen Christ, hear the proclamation of the uncompromised Word of God from the lips of one of the finest "comeback kids" in God's Kingdom, and see the demonstration of the Spirit with power, it is indeed a life-changing experience replete with the blessing of the Lord that makes rich and adds no sorrow. It is all because God laid hold of a man in the darkest season of his life, and turned his ashes into beauty, allowing him to be broken open so that he could feed the nations with the Bread of Heaven.

"Take plenty of time as you read this, feed on the rich morsels in each chapter, and let the Lord use Dr. Maiden's narrative and life-script as the strong meat of encouragement, so that you can rest assured that the same God who is the Author of his story, is the Author of yours as well. Prepare yourself. God has spread a table for you right here in this book in the presence of every enemy that wants to defeat you. Indeed, He is the God Of The Comeback, and it is time for yours to begin!

Dr. Mark J. Chironna
Church On The Living Edge
Mark Chironna Ministries, Orlando, Florida

INTRODUCTION

T his is my life's story. It's a story of the kindness and love of God to a broken and beaten man. It's the story of how the God of the Comeback can turn our greatest failures and setbacks into an opportunity for Him to give us a Comeback! Here's what this book will tell you:

- My childhood dream was always to serve God and His church.
- My wife and I began a church at the age of twenty-seven in Scottsdale, Arizona that God breathed on and blessed until it grew to thousands of members.
- Then as we were in mid-construction of a 4,800 seat auditorium, our church treasurer embezzled $20 million from us.
- This led to ten front-page headline stories about the church.
- Resulted in six lawsuits (two of them were class-action suits that were enjoined by several thousand people.).
- Meaning we had, at one point, fifteen concurrent attorneys representing the church and myself.

- This lead to the dramatic "growth" of the church from 4,000 to 140 people.
- We were forced into bankruptcy and lost the church property and our family's home.
- I became severely, manically depressed for over two years.
- My amazing oldest son turned to drugs due to all the pain he'd experienced.
- My family was homeless for a time.
- The federal government did an exhaustive, yearlong investigation into the church and my life, looking for any and all criminal wrongdoing --finding nothing in the end.
- The $20 million that was stolen was never returned.
- The man who stole the money went to prison.

But then . . . we started over with nothing but a promise from God. By His amazing grace and faithfulness, God gave us a second chance and an incredible Comeback in the same city that we had a massive public scandal. God has now given me double for all my trouble. He has given us a miracle, $30 million church facility debt free. Thousands of people are a part of the Church For The Nations family. We have eighteen church campuses around Arizona. Jesus healed me of depression, He set my son free and everything that I had lost, Jesus Christ has restored gloriously!

I believe my loving God can do the same for you. Because He is the God of the Comeback.

CHAPTER 1

Your Story Is Not Over!

We all want to be accepted and embraced by the people we know and the community we belong to. There seems to be an inner longing in our souls to be received and respected by others. Our search for acceptance becomes a guiding motivation in so many of the things we do and say in life.

This human desire for affirmation is a dominant part of our modern cultural mindset. It creates a pressure of enormous weight as things or people are deemed acceptable or unacceptable by its most current prognostications. This pressure can make a moral coward out of a great champion and a mindless follower out of a thoughtful leader.

Most of us would never face the violence of the force of public disapproval and rejection willingly. That is because perhaps the greatest singular human motivation is the avoidance of pain. We find it easier to sidestep around conflict and controversy to preserve our public profile before our families and communities. We do so many things out of the need and desire for acceptance. Accordingly then, many of our choices are tremendously influenced so that we can't accurately discern what may be the right or best thing we should do.

We have modern psychological terms and treatments for people who seem to not need social acceptance. They are considered abnormal or even potentially dangerous to the rest of society. This need to fit in, common to all mankind, begins in early childhood. It grows stronger in adolescence and peeks in or during teens. But does it ever just go away?

No, it doesn't.

But we learn as adults to better mask our disappointments and heartaches. We learn how to conceal how we feel about the personal rejections we experience.

It's easy to build a wall of indifference around our hearts because of past experiences. Our defense mechanism wants to prevent any future damage occurring, so we take the appropriate steps to preserve our delicate self-image.

But, what if, say, just like any other normal day, suddenly without any warning, our safe little world of acceptance and approval changed?

What would happen to us if abruptly we were thrust into the accusation and disapproval of our friends and community?

Would we survive such a crisis?

This happened to me.

I've learned a lot about myself and human nature through the most trying time of my life. These are some of the insights that emerged as my life's been shaken by an amazing series of circumstances. And let me begin by saying:

Your story isn't over!

No matter where you are or that you've been through, God is not done writing the script of your life! Though I write these pages, sharing many of the details of my journey and experience, the reality is that, ultimately, this is the testimony of how God worked to bring about an amazing comeback in my life. I can say with Paul:

> "But we have this treasure in earthen vessels, that the excellence of the power may be of God and not of us. We are hardpressed on every side, yet not crushed; we are perplexed, but not in despair; persecuted, but not forsaken; struck down, but not destroyed— always carrying about in the body the dying of the Lord Jesus, that the life of Jesus also may be manifested in our body. For we who live are always delivered to death for Jesus' sake, that the life of Jesus also may be manifested in our mortal flesh. So then death is working in us, but life in you."
> (2 Corinthians 4:7-12)

This book is my testament to the incredible grace and goodness of the God of the Comeback. It's important for you to understand and truly believe that the remarkable events that have transpired in my life aren't the result of my uniqueness or special standing with God. The remarkable things that have occurred in my life are entirely the result of the remarkable God we serve! If God can do these extraordinary things for me, He can do them for you, also. I believe that what God does for anyone, He'll do for everyone.

Being a minister doesn't qualify or disqualify me from being included or excluded from the normalcy of life or the intervention of God's healing and restoring grace. In other words, my vocation isn't the main factor in the outcome of my comeback story. This isn't the story of a minister with special standing and benefits with God. I'm just a man, just like other men, no better, no worse, but the same.

The position and partnership we have concerning our life's comeback are never being the sole author and main force required to make it happen, but to cooperate and participate with the direction, decisions, and actions that God invites us to take, whatever they may be.

We can't do it without God. God won't do it without us.

Hope is an amazing gift from God. When we are in possession of it, our souls become safely anchored against the raging storms of life. When we lack hope, the troubles and trials happening to us eventually become traumas and life altering and controlling disturbances in us. I pray that this book gives and increases real and life-changing hope for your life.

It doesn't matter how many people or events are working against you or have given up on you. God has not and never will give up on you! Don't let circumstances or your inward emotional reactions to them conspire to form an opinion and belief that God's forgotten or forsaken you. As Solomon prayed:

> "May the Lord our God be with us, as He was with our fathers. May He not leave us nor forsake us, that He may incline our hearts to Himself, to walk in all His ways, and to keep His commandments and His statutes and His judgments, which He commanded our fathers."
> (2 Kings 8:57, 58)

God hasn't left you, nor will He ever do so. God is not mad at you. He's unconditionally in love with you.

"Behold, I have indelibly imprinted (tattooed a picture of) you on the palm of each of My hands." (Isaiah 49:16; Amplified Bible)

Never give up on God, because He'll never give up on you. The greater the setback you've experienced in your life, the greater the opportunity for God to accomplish your comeback.

It's time for your comeback.

God's ready. Are you? Don't disqualify yourself for any reason. God's heard all our excuses before. They didn't stop Him then, and they won't stop Him now.

CHAPTER 2

The Beginning

My parents moved to Scottsdale, Arizona from Iowa when I as five years old and in kindergarten. They were devout Lutherans and quickly became leaders in the local Lutheran church. My dad owned an insurance agency that mushroomed very quickly to employ more than one hundred agents.

One Sunday a man from Campus Crusade for Christ, Eldon Priest, came to Abiding Savior Lutheran Church and shared the Four Spiritual Laws with the congregation. That Sunday, both of my parents accepted Jesus as their Savior and Lord after hearing the clear, simple and biblical presentation of the gospel. Somewhere in this same time frame, a wonderful children's leader at that church led me to Christ.

My parents dove into their newly discovered Christian life with great passion and commitment. In fact, the same day they received Christ, they went out in the streets of Scottsdale sharing the Four Spiritual Laws with others.

The story of how my folks became pastors is both amusing and sad. They started a Bible study Thursday nights for young people. This was precipitated by my uncle and cousin, who were drug-using, long-haired, sandal-wearing hippies, both receiving Christ. In just a few months our home became overrun with over a hundred young people (Jesus people) who found Christ and were hungry for more.

My dad, feeling a little overwhelmed by the number of young people, and the fact that he had no formal theological training, approached every church he knew of in the Phoenix metropolitan area and asked the pastors if he could bring a hundred hippies to church on Sunday. Without fail, every pastor responded the same, telling my father that, sure, the young people were welcome to their church, but only after all the men's hair was cut and beards were shaved, all the women had to wear dresses, and no sandals for either men or women were allowed.

After that universal response my mom and dad started their own church, New Life Chapel in Phoenix, Arizona. It was the early 70's and New Life grew to several hundred young people over the next couple of years.

As the church grew, my dad sought counsel from a prominent head pastor at the beginning of these events. This pastor told my father, "You can't be a businessman and serve the Lord." So the following day my father turned in the keys and relinquished all rights and future income from his large, highly successful agency. Let's just say that the standard of living at the Maiden household quickly changed.

I applaud my parents for their incredible faith and hunger to serve God. When my father quit, my parents started a Christian bookstore and suicide prevention hotline. And we made our home in the back of the bookstore for several years. I grew up near a large Native American reservation. with tons of "wide open spaces" that were perfect for exploring, having fun in and eventually running in. For those who have an interest, passion and ability to run, it can be a greatly enjoyable and rewarding experience. That's how it felt to me as I'd run through Arizona's beautiful Sonoran desert filled with cactus, desert trees and flowers, and hills and mountains. I have long legs and even as a boy, would take long strides while running. Several years later, during my junior and senior years of high school, my long legs and love of running would lead to three state championships in track.

But in the summer of my 12th year, my life was forever altered. I had taken off from our house on another desert run, this time a several mile journey across the reservation. All I can remember is enjoying a beautiful day while running on a seldom-used dirt road on the reservation. What happened next was truly a miraculous event. While running on that dirt road, as a skinny, long-legged young boy, my appendix burst and caused me to fall down unconscious on the side of that seldom traveled dirt road on the Pima Reservation.

I have no idea how long I laid there, completely unconscious, but it was for quite a while. Mind you, these dirt roads on the reservation can go days, weeks or even months without any traffic on them. My mother's brother, Greg, was a 20-something -year-old young man who had come to stay at our house for a while. He was a strung-out 'hippie' that my parents led to Christ and were discipling at our house. God gloriously delivered Uncle Greg from drugs, depression and several other harmful bondages. He had recently started a job in Mesa, a city southeast of Scottsdale. On the day that I 'passed out', Uncle Greg had decided to take a different route home from work in Mesa. He chose to explore the reservation and see if there was a road through it to our house.

He noticed a dirt road off the main roads and he just happened to turn down it to see where it led. About a mile down this lonely, dirt road, he thought he saw something lying on the road straight ahead. As he slowed down and stopped he suddenly realized that there was the body of a young boy, lying limp on the side of that road.

Instinctively, Uncle Greg leaped out of his car to investigate and offer help. After turning me over, to say that he was shocked that it was his young nephew would be quite an understatement. Realizing the gravity of the situation, Uncle Greg scooped me up in his arms, placed me in the passenger side of his car and sped home.

Here's where the story gets even more intriguing. My parents took me to the doctor several times over the next couple of weeks. I wasn't getting better, but losing more and more weight (I was a pretty skinny kid even before this happened). After several weeks filled with doctor appointments every couple of days, I was walking out of the doctor's office, walking as I had been since the first episode on the dirt road, leaning forward, unable to stand straight up, erect.

The doctor stopped me and asked why I was leaning forward. I said it was the only way I could walk. He repeatedly asked me to straighten up. I just couldn't. His face became flushed and his voice became urgent as he said to my mother, "We must operate on Mike immediately. Please take him to the hospital and I will meet you there."

In less than an hour and a half, I was in emergency surgery at Scottsdale Memorial Hospital. What our pediatrician had observed as I was leaving his office, unable to stand straight, was a symptom of an infected or burst appendix. After opening me up in the operating room, the surgical team realized my appendix had been burst for several weeks and that my life was in serious jeopardy.

They worked on me for hours and hours trying to do their best to remove the poison spilled from the burst appendix. I remember waking up the next day in a room by myself. There was two IVs in each arm and two tubes in my side. A machine was making a constant noise next to me. It was a pump connected to the tube that was continuing to drain the deadly, poisonous infection out of my body.

The worst part of my six week stay in intensive care was the shots I was given every few hours. They were filled with a powerful antibiotic and shot straight into my stomach. It wasn't the needle that was the issue, it was the unbearably excruciating pain I felt as the medicine made contact with the infection. When it was 'shot time' four or five nurses would come in together to hold me down during the slow delivery of the needed medicine to my very diseased, young body. The good thing was the lingering pain of these injections would usually diminish after 30 to 60 minutes.

I finally figured out the depth of the seriousness of my condition, when my parents began to parade relatives and pastors through my room. Hugs and tears from the loved ones, prayer from the pastors. I don't know the precise odds the doctors gave my folks, but it must have been pretty bad, especially at the beginning of my hospital stay. I had lived three weeks with a deadly poison cruising through my body. The doctors did everything they could. Now it would be entirely up to divine intervention whether or not I would live. I couldn't eat, and literally became skin and bones lying in the hospital bed.

Here's a funny story: I can laugh about it now after so many years. A few months before I was sick, I was with my parents in a second-hand store. At that time I had a little lawn business and had saved a little money. In that second hand store I found a shoebox filled with baseball cards for sale for $5.00. I bought the box of baseball cards and when I got home I began to look through it. I was extremely surprised and excited to discover what it contained: several featuring Babe Ruth, Ty Cobb, Mickey Mantle - you name it.

There were cards from the who's who of baseball lore. I had hit a gold mine and I knew it.

My parents had brought my cards to me in the hospital. After I became aware of the very real probability that I was going to die, I decided to bless a young boy down the hall who had a tonsillectomy with my pot of gold. I was dying and I wanted him to enjoy what God had blessed me to find. When you're dying, material things have little or no real value and importance to you. I still don't regret it to this day. I hope they were a blessing to that young man.

But I didn't die.

After the third or fourth week in the hospital, I began to do a little better each day. As it worked out, I was able to come home after almost two months, just before school started. God had sovereignly rescued me from death and any permanent physical disability. From then on, every day, week, month and year of my life would be the direct consequence of what the Lord did for me as a young boy.

As a young boy, I felt robbed of my summer, health, sports, etc. As a grown man, I look back and see the loving hand of God upon my life and its most vulnerable moments and my heart responds with genuine gratitude and thanksgiving.

As a young boy, I began to have incredible experiences with God, beginning around 11 or 12. Year by year I would feel the Lord speak to me about my future destiny to be a minister. Being the son of a pastor ever since I was a pre-teen boy, I felt the call of God to follow my father into the ministry. You know it's a call when you grow up in a pastor's home and see the harsh realities of the ministry and still want to be a pastor. I knew it was God's call for me, the right path for me to begin walking on. So strong and consistent were these moments and their cumulative impact that I entered seminary right out of high school. My father was a friend of Jack Hayford, and that year Pastor Hayford became the president of Life Bible College in Glendale, California. After a phone call, that's where I ended up going.

In the spring of my freshman year of Bible college, I came home on break to see my family and attend my parent's church. When I walked into the church office, sitting at the reception table was the most beautiful girl I had ever seen, Mary Murawa.

Let me backtrack a little. I had made a promise to God that I would not date any woman who wasn't going to be my wife. So, after attending seminary, where dating was such an important part of these young people's lives, I refused to do so. I would prayerfully seek God when someone acted interested in me, or I felt an attraction to them. For months all I heard from God, after many opportunities, was "No."

But things changed. After seeing the stunningly attractive Mary at my father's church, I returned to school and spent time praying (and pinning) over her. I felt I had the answer. It was "Yes."

That summer I couldn't wait for school to end so I could get home and form a relationship with this young woman. As it happened, I ended up working at the hotline in the same building where Mary worked for my father. I was assured that God must have placed the same interest and attraction in her for me as I had for her, but after being "shot down" five times in attempts to go on a date, I began to have my doubts.

Then one day, on my way to lunch, I stopped by her desk and casually invited her to join me. Unbelievably, she said, "Yes!"

I took her to Macayo's Mexican restaurant and for an hour talked her ear off about God, life and marriage. That's right, on the first date I talked about marriage. I knew she was the one. Fortunatley, soon she did too.

Going back to college without Mary was torturous. Three of us went to college from the church, all with girl-friends or finances. Within a few weeks, only Mary and I were still together. We actually grew very close over that year and I see the value in our relationship being "tested" during that time. I wrote her every day. (The phone company came and removed the phone from my apartment after the first month - something about a huge bill!)

Fast forward a few years and we were married at 21. Thirteen months later we had our first baby, Melody Joy, and eighteen months after her, our second child, Matthew James. During those years I served in churches as a youth pastor, worship pastor and then associate pastor. But they were not easy times financially. It was necessary for me to also work outside the church because of the inability to receive a salary, or much of one, from the church. God taught me so much about everything during this time. In my last part time job, I made $2,000 a week on straight commission, working only 15-20 hours a week because of my full-time (but non-sala-ried) position at the church.

In 1984, the elders of the church where I worked, where my father was the senior pastor, approached me in secret and asked me to take over the senior pastoral position. They were ousting my father. Stunned, I immediately declined and real-ized I needed to do something else. I resigned my position and began to seek God.

CHAPTER 3

Grumpy Old Men

After much prayer, Mary and I and our two children, Melody and Matthew, moved back to Phoenix from Orange County, California in February of 1985 to pioneer a church called Eagle's Nest Christian Fellowship. We had a powerful assurance from the Lord that, even though we were both only 27 at the time, we were to plant a church in the valley, so we packed up by faith, rented a house, sight unseen, and moved out to Phoenix. A small church there needed a pastor, so we, merged with that tiny group in the beginning of the Eagle's Nest. We grew to about 150 by the end of the first year and moved into a commercial building in the Scottsdale Airpark in 1986.

There is only one church in the earth consisting of every born again believer in Jesus Christ. There is only "one church" in Phoenix and in spite of many different meeting places and denominations, God sees us all as "one." I've always believed that and so it was only natural for me to attempt to seek and build relationships with other believers, pastors and leaders in the Phoenix area. Most important to me was to build relationships with the spiritual fathers God had raised up and was using in this area.

Acting on this impulse, I called and scheduled meetings with two of the pastors of the largest churches whose influence was recognized by the church in the city and beyond. I had the heart of a "son" and wanted to open my life to accountability and mentorship to both of these men of God. I had no desire to be a "lone ranger," and because our church was "nondenominational," I was seeking to build the necessary relationships every young leader needs to succeed in their destiny.

Driving up to the huge megachurch on the day of my first appointment with one of these leading pastors, I was genuinely excited and filled with anticipation about forming a father and son relationship with him. I felt only joy looking at his incredible buildings and property. We were on the same team. His victories were victories for all of God's people and I found it easy to rejoice for what God had done through this mighty man of God. Our new church was many miles away from his church's location. We were in an area that desperately needed churches and our goal was to reach those who needed Christ and a church home.

Walking into his office, the pastor stood up, came out from behind his desk and shook my hand. As we both sat down I felt like a student sitting at the feet of a great teacher, so ready to learn, grow and be fathered. But none of those things happened that day.

After some polite pleasantries, with questions about my family and the church, the conversation suddenly took an unexpected, and entirely unfortunate turn in a different direction. Looking right at me, he said, "I give your church less than a year until you fail, shut down and leave town."

He had no words of encouragement or wisdom, only a pronouncement of doom and failure. That was it, he was done. I was stunned. He got up, shook my hand again, led me out of his office, said, "Good-bye," and closed the door.

I was in shock as I walked past the receptionist and other employees. I some how made my way back to my car. Climbing in, I just sat there for awhile, brokenhearted and confused. If not for the powerful confidence and confirmations Mary and I had about pastoring in this city, I'm not sure we could have survived that unexpected blow.

We cried together and prayed and moved on.

The good thing for us was that I had scheduled an appointment with the other leading pastor and spiritual father the following week. Driving up to his church, I couldn't help but feel real anticipation about what this day would hold for my life and church as we "connected" with a powerful 'general' in the Kingdom of God. I was a son searching for a spiritual father, and even after being harshly treated and rejected by one, I was certain things would be different this time. Both of these men were over 30 years older than me and had been used to build great churches for the Lord.

Walking into the office of this highly acclaimed leader was, once again, a moment of rejoicing for all God had done through his life and a moment of expectation for what the Lord would say and impart to me that day. His greeting was very cordial and sincere. This was a good man, a family man, a godly man. He asked me questions about my life, family and church for a few minutes. I shared my heart as a young pastor, my dream to build a great church in Scottsdale (many miles from his church), my desire to be "fathered" and mentored.

Now it was his time to pour into me. I was ready and open for anything God would say through him. I wasn't ready for what happened next.

"Young man, I admire your zeal and passion, but I give you about six months until you close the church down."

It felt like I was reliving the nightmare from two weeks before. He couldn't find it in himself to say anything positive, hopeful or encouraging. He just wanted me out of the way and out of' his town. The only church he cared about in the city was his church.

My reaction was different this time. Once again, here I sat in the parking lot of a 'mega' church after being brutally disappointed by a negative and hurtful personal encounter with the senior pastor. I knew these men were both men of God, and it seemed like an unfathomable contradiction to me that both men's response was so un-Christlike. What in the 'bleep' had just happened?

Sitting there, I began to get angry, angry at two "grumpy old men" who couldn't find it within themselves to bless and encourage someone at the beginning of their journey. My thoughts began to run wild with criticisms and judgments toward these two men, whose behavior was grossly inappropriate and ungodly. I was growing angrier and angrier as I came into a clearer picture of what had happened. What on earth is wrong with these old men?

As I was stewing in anger something quite remarkable occurred. God began to speak and deal with me. Here's what He said to me that changed my life forever: "Son, someday you'll be the 'old man' sitting behind the big desk and young pastors and leaders will come to you seeking guidance, wisdom and encouragement. If you don 't deal with all the hurt and pain that you'll experience between now and then, by the time you have been given a platform of influence, instead of being an encouragement, support and blessing to others, you'll discourage and hurt them."

Wow. God was giving me an incredibly vivid picture and life lesson through what I'd endured with these two "grumpy old men." I realized that "hurt people hurt people!" These two men were good men, God's men, but because they hadn't properly processed and recovered from their own disappointments and wounds, they were unable to give something they didn't have.

Now that I'm the age of those men, thirty years later, I'm more determined than ever to never become a "grumpy old man" in the ministry or to my family and others.

No matter what difficulties or disappointments we face in life, we can know with great assurance that Jesus Christ heals our lives! "I have come to heal the brokenhearted" and there's nothing or no one He can't heal today.

Soon after Mary and I began the Eagle's Nest in 1985, we began to have a steady stream of visitors from one large central Phoenix church. Although our church was in north Scottsdale, almost every week while I greeted visitors, several families would introduce themselves as being members of this large and historic church, a very prominent church in the Phoenix area..

Recognizing a pattern and wanting understanding about the cause for the consistency of families from this church, we began to ask them, "Why us? Why did you come to the Eagle's Nest?"

I have to admit, that to this day, I'm still astonished at the common answer from dozens of visitors. "Our pastor talks about you almost every week from the pulpit. He tells us, "We're not like the Eagle's Nest. We don't believe in what they're doing and how they' re doing it. Stay away from Mike Maiden and the Eagle's Nest Church."

Whenever we hear the criticisms of others about our lives, and in this case, my church, it's never a pleasant experience and feeling. My first thought was, I'd never even met their pastor. Our church was a great distance from his. Why would someone I've never met continually and very publicly wage war against me and the church? Finding out you have a real enemy who despises everything about you and is working to destroy you is very disappointing and saddening.

The way it worked was every time he talked about us, the next couple of Sundays several visitors would come from the big church. We call this 'reverse psychology' where we feel almost compelled to do what we're commanded not to. I immediately tried to secure a meeting, but was repeatedly rejected. It escalated when his pastoral staff began to 'sneak' over themselves to get a firsthand glimpse of the church their pastor couldn't stop waging war against.

I'm writing this chapter from his former desk, in his former office, located at his former church, that once prominent church. In 2009, the debt free church property was GIVEN TO OUR CHURCH! Seated on thirteen acres in a beautiful, established and wealthy neighborhood, consisting of 135,000 square feet of buildings on a major and well-known street, with a sanctuary that seats over 2,400 people. In the Phoenix metropolitan area, the fifth largest urban area in the USA with a population of 4.5 million people, there are several thousand churches and several thousand church buildings. The fact that God would sovereignly turn over to us the very property built and pastored by a man filled with unbelievable hostility and hatred for us, who waged a personal 'jihad' against us for decades, is unbelievably miraculous! I've never asked God for this property. I've never 'wished' or coveted that we could have it. I didn't know really anything about it and it literally never crossed my mind to consider this as a home for our church.

What is God saying through this public parable to this city and His people everywhere? That He is able to vindicate His people and servants without their vengeful attitudes or actions. That God can give you, in the power of one miraculous moment, property, wealth, favor, influence, restoration and breakthrough.

Every time as I drive up Central Avenue, a beautiful tree-laden street, and turn into our 'miracle building;' I am deeply humbled and awestruck by the kindness and greatness of my God. Now to the bigger picture of why God did what He's done with giving us this multi-million dollar property. As I was initially dreaming and praying, when the possibility of receiving this property was first revealed, I had an important and tremendously instructive revelation from God. Sitting in the massive, but empty parking lot of the church, praying about the future, I had a vision of a well. It was like those old-fashioned ones you see in movies, made of stone, about four feet high. It was literally overflowing with garbage; tires, junk, trash, and dirt. The Lord simply said to me, "Son, I don't want you to do anything new. I want you to let me finish the business I have for this property and this city. Unstop the well that is already here and let the living waters of my Spirit flow out to this city and to all the nations."

Wow! I got it. God wanted me to "take the baton" from a former generation and finish the race. God has a redemptive purpose for every family, city and nation. In every family, city and nation God has unfinished business that He is passionately wanting and patiently waiting to fulfill. I see the beautiful continuum of God's purpose for this city in what's transpired. The waters are flowing again. The church is filled with God's presence and power again. Thousands are coming to the oasis that heaven has opened once again.

I wonder what the unfinished business is that God longs to complete in your life and family? Either by knowing some of our family history or by the revelation of the Holy Spirit, we can be given keen insight into what God wanted and tried to do through former generations. Often we can see the destructive work of the enemy in robbing family members from some heavenly purpose and blessing. Many individuals and families live paralyzed in a perpetual sadness or discouragement over the failure and devastation of previous generations.

I suppose for several years many of the former members, as they would drive by and see their church being almost totally unused (attendance had dropped to sixty-three people when it was given to us) or think of what the church used to be and what it had now become, they would feel genuine sorrow about all that was lost. But now what God is doing is even better than the 'good old days' of the past!

In your life and family it's time for God's unfinished business to be fulfilled! God wants to bring a supernatural restoration to areas that have been devastated by loss! He wants to 'move the ball forward' by not just giving you back something that you've lost and the enemy stole, He wants to advance his purpose and promise to your life and family to what He's destined! Yes, not just a 'recovery,' but great advancement and progress!

No matter how dysfunctional a family, or how oppressed a city or nation, God has embedded an eternal, divine purpose for their existence. When we seek God about our families, cities and nations, He will reveal the predestined, redemptive purpose for them. Kingdom' Success' is always attached to the fulfilling of Kingdom 'Purpose.' It's not really about us, it's all about His purposes for this world. I love to help hurting and broken people and places discover their divine purpose and experience a divine restoration. What someone or something is now, may not be anything like what God's created and called them to be. When we can see them like God does, it changes everything!

I think it is almost impossible to fully prepare someone for the ministry. Although growing up in a minister's home, attending seminary and being "hands on" in ministry at an early age did give me a head start compared to most pastors, I wasn't full prepared. Remarkably, despite all the stops and starts, that little church we pioneered in 1985 began to grow and grow and grow. In fact it more than doubled in size for several years in a row. It grew from a few dozen, to a few hundred, to a few thousand. For ten straight years, every year, the church grew numerically, financially and organizationally. We constantly marveled at God's continual blessing upon us.

As long as I can remember I've been driven by a need to achieve and succeed. As a young man I used athletics to channel this drive and discipline into. I hated to lose and would do whatever it took in order to achieve victory. In both high school, then college, I was what they called an overachiever. That means I made up for a lack of superior physical ability by outworking and outthinking my fellow competitors.

I had no way of knowing then what I know now, that my hunger for achievement was based upon my need for acceptance. I found it rewarding to be known as a successful athlete. In fact I built by own self-identity around my successes in athletics. (I could do this because I had many more personal successes than defeats.) Through athletic achievement, popularity and respect followed as the spoils of victory.

My drive for achievement and success was now being fulfilled by the success of the church I pastored. People began to identify me as the pastor of a huge, growing church. I found my public image of being a seemingly highly successful pastor became my own self-portrait of who I was as a person. Michael Maiden the successful athlete was now Michael Maiden the successful professional. My self-image, self-worth and self-esteem were all centered around my professional accomplishments.

As I said before, this is the way I had always lived. I would capture a prize or achievement, then use its significance to give meaning and value to my life. I was the husband of an extraordinarily attractive wife, the father of four beautiful children and the pastor of a great church. It seemed that all the pieces had come into place to give my life a true sense of value and meaning.

To thousands of people, I was respected. Appreciation became the oxygen I needed to live. To be needed and respected in the very city I grew up as a child, I was having my dream come true.

By 1990, the church was over a thousand in attendance, and was in need of a worship leader. For most of those years I continued to be the primary worship leader along with being the lead pastor. On my way home from church one Sunday I began to complain about the quality and musical competency of the worship leader (me) and the team I worked with. As I drove past a little bar called The Dirty Drummer, I said to the Lord, "They've got better singers and musicians in that little bar singing to 20 drunks than we do in the church, ministering to thousands."

When I got home I had an incredible moment with God when I heard him say, "Why don't you do something about it?"

I was immediately stunned by the possibility that the inferior level of music in our church was my fault, not God's! The Lord then spoke to my heart, "Pray for talented singers and musicians to come out of darkness into My kingdom."

Wow. I never realized how simple the solution was to a problem that had bothered me for several years. I dropped to my knees in our living room and began to pray, as the Lord had said, for the salvation of musicians. While I'm praying, our home phone rang in the kitchen. I got up and answered it and on the other end was my childhood best friend, also a P.K. (preacher's kid) who had moved to Hollywood and become a well-known and respected musician and composer there. It was a clear sign to me of God's eagerness to help with our music.

What happened next is truly extraordinary. The owners of the largest jazz nightclub in Arizona, Jim and Nancy Simmons, were both radically converted to Christ. When they would come to church, they'd bring with some of the greatest musicians in our city and they'd all fill a whole row at church.

I'm not a rocket scientist, but it didn't take me long to connect the dots. I soon asked them—and they accepted—to be a part of the Eagle's Nest worship team. Literally overnight, the quality of our music went from being mediocre and average, to being off the charts.

We had a great team, but we still needed a person to lead it and be our worship leader. During this time I had prayed, prophesied and ministered to a young, nineteen year old, struggling pastor's son named Israel Houghton. He was beaten up, demoralized and vulnerable, but God began to heal, restore and strengthen his young life.

During prayer one day, I felt the Lord say plainly that I was to mentor and hire Israel to be our new worship pastor.

I have to admit, this was a hard thing to digest. He wasn't yet a competent musician and he only knew one worship song. I couldn't escape the leading of the Holy Spirit to pull the trigger, so in spite of his age, his musical ability, even his color—black (Eagle's Nest was over 90% white at that time)—I hired Israel.

What happened next was predictable: It shook the church. Some people thought I'd lost my mind. We had been interviewing some of the best worship leaders in the country before hiring Israel. A group did leave: some because they were prejudice, some because of Israel's limited ability at that time and some because they'd lost faith in my leadership for hiring him.

They all were wrong. Israel began to grow spiritually, musically and personally. Within a few months, the improvement was evident. All I had asked from the church was a few months of trust -time for Israel to grow.

By the second year, he was beginning to bloom and could do other people's songs as well as they could. By the third year, his creative songwriting gift began to develop more and more. In the fourth year, 1994, we did an international television program on TBN called "Shower of Power." Twenty-five years later, Israel has won six Grammy awards and is one of the most successful songwriting, worship leaders in the world. Israel's story was a metaphor for the Eagle's Nest - a true "rags to riches" story of God's goodness and grace. Here's a few other world-class worship leaders that were born out of that season: Ricardo Sanchez, George Chadwick, and B.J. Putnam.

Almost unbelievably, at the same time we were blessed with a new property for a new church building in Scottsdale and, by our seventh anniversary, Eagle's Nest had grown to over 3,000 actual attenders.

Reflecting back on those days, I am overwhelmed in a sense of God's kindness and mercy. I didn't know what I was doing most of the time (still don't!). But God blessed and used us to accomplish much for His Kingdom around the world. I only wish I had appreciated it back then as much as I do now.

Have you ever had the feeling or sensation that you were running away from something that was chasing after you? All while I was being driven to achievement in order to obtain acceptance, I had felt as if I was losing ground to kind of an inner void that was beginning to occupy more and more ground in my conscience. Success is a bittersweet experience when you try to build your life on it. It's a fleeting sensation that offers no lasting contentment but instead requires more and more achievement to meet the needs of a unsatisfied soul.

With lingering questions in the back of my mind I often wondered why I wasn't more happy and content with the circumstances of my life. But just like most other men and women who are under the intoxication of their success, I was deaf to the cry of my own heart, until a second major life changing event took place.

CHAPTER 4

I Lived One Way For So Long, Not Knowing It Was Wrong

S tepping back for a moment, in 1988 our church was three years old. God was moving and blessing us and we were growing. At the end of a Sunday morning service, after praying over those who came to the altar, I noticed a man who was patiently waiting to meet me. As I walked towards him, he reached out his hand and said, "Hello Pastor Maiden, my name is Hank and God sent me here to help build your church."

Those words were like music to my ears as a young pastor. Over the next seven years, Hank became a vitally important and visible part of the leadership of the church. He started our benevolence fund and our widows' fund. He and his wife were generous and helpful in so many ways. His business seemed to be growing exponentially just like our church, often doubling in size from year to year. He drove a Mercedes, owned a jet and lived in a mansion. Hank started several businesses and had many well-known people as clients who spoke very highly of him. People in the church who did business with him often praised and endorsed him for his character and results.

At the time, it only then seemed natural to me to ask Hank to act as an unpaid "church treasurer" and oversee our newly begun building program. Around our seventh anniversary, we had purchased seventeen acres on the busiest street in Scottsdale. We had also begun the construction of a 4,800 seat auditorium at this prime location. I had always felt unqualified and burdened by the financial business of the church. I just wanted to seek God and minister to people and was eager to turn the finances over to someone I thought was completely trustworthy. That person was Hank.

But I was wrong. I made a horrible mistake. Hank was running a long-term Ponzi scheme for over eight years and every one of his 6 or 7 businesses was nothing but a front to cover his illegal activity.

In the late summer of 1995, while our attendance was booming and our building ready to be finished, Hank was indicted by the government and exposed in the press for who he really was: a con man who had stolen $20 million dollars from his clients and families in our church. I had a few weeks warning before everything went public, when, for the first time, several church members had called me. Their monthly checks from their investment with Hank hadn't come in and when they called him to find out what was happening, Hank wouldn't speak to them.

I immediately called Hank and asked him what was going on to create this trouble. Hank interrupted me, unleashed a profane verbal attack and then hung up. Shocked and saddened I stared at the phone for a long time trying to process what had just happened. In my heart I knew now who he was, even though it would take my mind several more weeks to agree.

It all broke loose one Sunday, in August of 1995. I was excited about delivering a brand new message to the church that Sunday morning. We had several Sunday services and I was looking forward to having another spiritually and personally rewarding Sunday. The crowds of people that came to every service seemed to validate my worth to the church and community. On Sundays, as a custom, I never read the newspaper before I'd minister. My mind was too preoccupied with the message I'd worked on, I didn't want to lose my mental focus. But this Sunday there wasn't even a morning paper outside our house. One of my thoughtful church members had come and picked it up.

After the morning services, my wife and a few of my staff, gently approached me to give me the most shocking news of my life: my church and I were on the front page of the Sunday morning paper. It wasn't good news. Hank was being investigated for fraud and the article was all about the Ponzi scheme, his church involvement (including pictures of him and our church building) and activities. Although the article was filled with many—over thirty—factual inaccuracies, the general theme was correct.

As I read the first article, I was astonished they could say so many things about me and the church that were completely and factually untrue. The inference was: look at this church, it's building the biggest building in Scottsdale, raising millions of dollars, and look at who has just stolen $20 million: he must have put it all in the church. That wasn't true and could be easily disproven (we had been approved for a $12 million loan). That didn't stop them from inferring it over and over again.

The newspaper inferred that if he was like that, then the church and I must be a den of iniquity, the old "birds of a feather flock together" idea. Over the next several months this particular paper did at least ten front-page negative stores on the church. I found out later that several angry ex-church members were personally overseeing every article written.

Let me try to explain some personal dynamics of what was happening to me. As I was growing up I gave myself completely to the Lord at a young age. The Lord kept me from smoking or drinking or using drugs. I met my wife while I was still a teenager and had lived a morally pure life. Because of the way I had grown up as a child and lived as an adult, I thought that I was protected from trouble.

I was wrong.

I sat in my chair and stared at the article written about the church and me. How could this happen to me? How could I lose my public reputation after building it for almost twenty years? Couldn't people discern that I wasn't like that other man and that the church wasn't what the paper said it was? It seemed that what I had worked so hard my entire life to build was destroyed in just one day.

At the beginning, most of the church stood with us. But this was no normal storm. It lasted for several years and it destroyed everything in its path. Hundreds of members left the church along with some key staff. It's hard for any church to endure just one powerful public hit, let alone months and months of media bashing. One TV station followed up on the newspaper article with another couple of stories. People had lost money with a man who was an important and visible leader in our church. This man came highly recommended by national Christian leaders to my church. For many years he faithfully served at our church before he as given a leadership position.

But he wasn't what I thought he was.

And people wanted blood.

It's a horrible experience to watch something or someone you love die. But at the same time the church was being shaken, I was being shaken to the very depth of my being. My world began to crumble. I had never experienced a defeat as devastating as this. My self-image was shattered into a thousand tiny pieces. My reputation was not only lost, but ruined. I was now the pastor of a church involved in scandal. The thing I feared most had come upon me.

I had built my life on the perceived value of my achievements and my life was now lost without any positive identity. This powerful truth became very real to me: if your life is built on people's approval, it can be destroyed by their rejection. If you allow people to build you, people can break you.

As more and more members of the church left, my self-worth and identity shattered with every bad report I received. I realize now I had built my life on a lie that I had value and meaning because people gave it to me. I needed to realize that:

GOD VALUES ME EVEN WHEN PEOPLE DON'T.
GOD ACCEPTS ME EVEN WHEN PEOPLE DON'T.
GOD LOVES ME EVEN WHEN PEOPLE DON'T.

CHAPTER 5

When People Lose Their Money, They Lose Their Minds

I was very upset. To be honest, I was upset with God. How and why could He let this happen to me? I was also upset with myself. If I was walking so carefully how could I be so foolish?

When I finished reading the first newspaper article I honestly thought my life was over. My value and purpose as a leader seemed permanently destroyed. In my heart that day I heard the Lord speak to me.

It went something like this:

LORD: "Michael, why are you so upset?"

ME: "Haven't you read the paper today Lord?"

LORD: "Yes, but why are you so unhappy?"

ME: "Lord, because I just had my reputation stripped away from me"

LORD: "It was taken because you wouldn't give it up. I don't need your reputation. I need your heart."

I realized that very moment that I was more upset about losing my reputation, my public persona, than about anything else. I had spent so many years building and maintaining my reputation that it had now become a stumbling block between the Lord and me and his continuing purpose for my life.

In my heart I knew who I was and I knew God knew who I was, but I had never derived much satisfaction from just that. I was used to feeding off the value that people placed up my life. When that food supply of positive public opinion was suddenly cut off, I began to starve. I began to search. I began to weep.

Was I more concerned in maintaining the affection and approval of people or of God? I realized that day:

THE ONLY OPINION OF YOU
THAT MATTERS IS GOD'S.

I could no longer build my life upon the need for widespread acceptance and respect. I had lost the power to do that. It was time to re-build my life, my self-worth, self-esteem, and self-image, by my relationship with God and Him alone.

Almost immediately, before any kind of clarity would come on what had happened and who was ultimately responsible, the legal avalanche began. People wanted their money back and the church was very vulnerable because of Hank's prominence, our size, buildings and assumed wealth. What people didn't know is that the church lost more with Hank than anyone. We literally had nothing left, but the lawsuits came anyway—six of them—of which two were class action. Because of the nature of our judicial system and its tremendous complexities, I was required to have different lawyers for every different legal situation, which ended up being fifteen, all at one time, each lawyer representing a pressing legal problem. I was forced to deal with this new reality, our new normal, speaking and meeting with fifteen lawyers each week and often several times every day.

I had never had any personal or even vocational legal difficulties before this time. To be suddenly dropped into the harshness, violence and ungodliness of our legal system was one of the most demoralizing and traumatic experiences of my life. For example, I had a judge in his private quarters literally curse and scream at me for being a minister and a Christian, then storm off after recusing himself from our case.

One lawyer called us and demanded a million dollars by the end of the week or else he'd have the paper write another front-page story about us. We didn't have the money, nor did we steal his client's money, so we immediately said, "No" to his demand. Two days later, the Scottsdale Tribune published an article, including front-page headlines that were completely false. It was shocking to see the collaboration and the fearlessness of the press to publish what was easily proven to be untrue allegations.

In the midst of the unyielding legal and media firestorm, I received a disturbing phone call. It was the U.S. State Attorney General for Arizona asking for a meeting. I immediately complied and we scheduled one for the next day. I walked into the federal building and took the elevator up to the Attorney General's office floor.

After introducing myself to the security personnel there, I was led into a large conference room. Sitting around a beautiful, wooden conference table were twelve or thirteen people, who then began to introduce themselves: the U.S. Attorney General, State Attorney General, State FBI director,

County Attorney, etc. They all seemed genuinely surprised that I showed up and that I had no legal representation. My attitude was, I was innocent and had nothing to hide.

Several hours later, as the meeting concluded, one of the persons there privately pulled me to the side and said, "Pastor, you need a lawyer." I called Jay Sekulow, who gave me good advice on finding an appropriate legal representative. We found and hired Ed Novak who was one of the top criminal attorneys in Arizona.

Attorney Novak scheduled some meetings and made some phone calls and then met with Mary and I. He told us that the government knew, with certainty, that Hank was a criminal. They were convinced I was one, too, because of our long-standing relationship with him.

When you're a law-abiding citizen with not even a speeding ticket in your past, and then the most powerful governmental personnel and agencies say they're convinced of your guilt, it was like a horrible nightmare that I couldn't awake from. I told my lawyer I was innocent and that I would cooperate 100% with anyone and everyone to prove it.

Shortly thereafter, the government subpoenaed and we eagerly complied to the delivery of over 300,000 documents from the church, our complete financial history. It took over a year, but one day they called and asked us where to deliver a truckload of 300,000 documents.

They were all done. They had found nothing. The Attorney General sent a letter to our lawyer, "We know Pastor Maiden's innocent, but we think he's foolish for who he trusted."

A year of tremendous intensity, stress and uncertainty was suddenly over without a whimper.

During that dark season, our family had our phones tapped, garbage gone through, and received anonymous death threats. An influential person involved with the investigation privately told me, "When we couldn't find what we were looking for - financial improprieties with the church or any connection to Hank - we then started looking for anything else, big or very small that would justify our continued investigation. After an exhaustingly thorough examination of your life and church, the only surprise we found was that you and your wife like to go to the movies."

After being ravaged in the press and assaulted in the courts, it seemed like the truth was finally beginning to eek out. The very sad and maddening reality of the legal battles was that many of those in the system view it as some kind of game. For those of us who've had the unwanted and unfortunate experience of being in the grip of a legal struggle, it isn't a game, but a traumatic life affecting and altering experience.

Shortly into the preparations for our legal defense in the lawsuits, something quite unexpected and extremely unfortunate took place. Both of the insurance companies the church had, whose policies included providing and paying for lawyers if we ever faced any legal action, at almost the exact time, sued the church, attempting to break their contracts and all contractual obligations. The church could not afford to pay for fifteen contemporaneous attorneys.

Having no way to continue our defense while now having to contest with the insurance companies, we were left with one onerous and tragic course of action: filing bankruptcy as a church. The disappointment I felt being forced into this action was monumental. All of our lawyers said they fully expected us to win the law suits, but now we were forced to suspend our defense and file for Chapter 11 bankruptcy.

As a young man and pastor, I had formed a very negative and even judgmental attitude towards the idea of bankruptcy and those who employed it in their life or business.

Even though a Chapter 11 bankruptcy is quite different, as it allows the repayment of debt and the eventual restoration of a corporate credit, it was still bankruptcy. Most people who would hear the news, would say now that "the church went bankrupt."

Up to this point, I had been fighting with all my strength to protect and preserve the church, but something in me began to die as the realization of what had and was happening. It began to set in: no matter how hard I had worked and fought to 'save' the church, I was going to fail. Not just any kind of failure, a spectacularly public and epic failure. The kind that the public talk about, and, boy, were people ever talking. From their pulpits, pastors would make broad and general statements about us, that they were sure were true, because they either read it in the paper or heard it from someone who said they were there.

I got a call from one of our lawyers and even though he was suspended from continuing our legal defense, he asked for a meeting with me and I obliged. He was a devoted Catholic and for some reason he took a special interest in us "Protestants." As I entered his office, he had every wall covered with paper and a blackboard sitting in the middle of the room. After he politely greeted me, he asked me to take a seat. Then for the next few hours he proceeded to show me an incredibly detailed and factually true narrative of the past ten years of our church. Pointing, one by one, to the hundreds of documents, news clippings and his own notes, he began to give an unbelievably accurate history of my life and church. Painstakingly revealing and explaining how con men maneuver and manipulate their way into other's lives and how it had happened to us. He covered everything. It was like having a three-day complete medical evaluation in its incredible detail and thoroughness. Only this was not a doctor's office, it was a lawyer who we were no longer able to even retain.

After sitting there for almost two hours, feeling like I had just been through a "This is Your Life" episode, he then gave his most dramatic and heartfelt summation at closing: "Pastor Michael, you are a good and godly man who completely trusted a professional con man. That's what con men do: they win people's confidence so they can steal their money or possessions. You are an innocent man."

For months, so much pain I had experienced by the hands of lawyers in court, depositions, and lawsuits, I was now being incredibly comforted and powerfully ministered to in the most profound way possible. He wasn't a pastor or counselor or some other therapeutic agent. He was a lawyer who took it upon himself to help a lost young pastor find his way again. I was seriously shocked by whowhom God had used, (a Catholic lawyer) to bring clarity and healing to my life. Out of the fifteen lawyers that were so much a part of my life for several years, two of them were kind and caring, including this lovely Catholic man.

People are amazing. Some of the stories and rumors that I've heard about the church and me made me want to be afraid of myself! Christians seem to be especially good at spreading bad reports that get worse with every telling. My original plan for this book was to give a detailed explanation and defense by telling my side of the story. But one day I heard the Lord whisper this to my heart: "If you defend yourself, I won't. If I defend you, you won't have to."

I entered into a season of deep brokenness and constant repentance. Not for the reasons that some would like to think, but God began to accomplish a deep inner work in my heart, helping me see how so many of the attitudes I had about people and the ministry were wrong.

I've also learned something about not being so quick to judge other people that are in trying circumstances of any kind. I think maybe that it is the hurting that eventually make the best healers.

I've written several books now, most of them expounded on what I believed to be important scriptural principals. They were written to teach a truth or truths I had discovered from God's word. This book is entirely different. It is the free-flowing dialogue of my heart through the experiences that have re-shaped my life.

Integrity is when we become brutally honest about our lives, to God, to ourselves, and to others. Integrity is a sincere honesty of heart and mind. We live in a generation that places greater value upon style that substance, upon perception than reality, upon personal reputation more that personal integrity. But if you're in any kind of public or private conflict, the secret weapon of eventual success will be your integrity.

In the Bible there are two striking examples of integrity and the lack of integrity in the life of the first two kings of Israel, Saul and David.

Saul was chosen to be king by both God and the people. He was physically gifted and seemed like the perfect choice. His reign began with a series of victories until one day he faced a decision that would reveal his fatal weakness. He was sent by God's commandment to completely destroy the Amalekite nation. God had been waiting for a very long time to bring judgment against this nation for their cruel and destructive treatment of Israel for generations.

Saul went about this task but when he saw the wealth and resources of the conquered nation, he kept the best for himself and Israel. God's directions were to completely destroy everything of that nation. Saul compromised by keeping the best and destroying the rest. This solution seemed like a reasonable compromise to King Saul. But compromise is the cancer that destroys integrity.

God immediately dispatches his main mouthpiece, the prophet Samuel, to confront Saul about his compromise and disobedience. Upon being confronted, King Saul initially issues a strong denial but eventually admits to his actions. God issues a strong judgment against Saul for his sin. Saul seems unaffected by the promised judgment and asks the prophet to come out to the balcony with him and publicly bless him. Saul's concern was not for his standing with God, it was for his standing with the people. He would rather have kept his reputation with man than his integrity with God.

With God's presence now absent from his life, and with a growing public disapproval of his leadership, Saul descends into a spiral of depression and self-destruction. He dies by his own hands in suicide, the ultimate act of self-hatred. When you use the approval of people to build your life, the rejection of people will destroy your life.

When God's approval builds on our life, people's rejection can't destroy us.

As just a young teenage boy, the youngest son of eight brothers, David the son of Jesse, was quietly anointed to be the next king. In short order he then defeated the monstrous giant Goliath and was "hired" to play his harp in King Saul's palace. But the insecurity of King Saul led to irrational accusations and attacks that culminated in a plot to murder him. David was now running for his life as the most wanted criminal in all of Israel. He was unjustly accused and persecuted for over a decade by an insanely jealous King Saul. David lost his reputation.

Twice during Saul's search to find and kill David, the most remarkable thing happened. King Saul walked right into the cave where David was hiding with some men. Saul was alone and vulnerable. Both times David restrained his anger and overcame his sense of injustice, and refused to lay a hand on his tormentor. Instead he put his trust and defense in the hands of God. He kept his integrity.

Later in his life as the King of Israel, God sends the prophet Nathan to confront David on his, up to then, secret sin. David had committed murder and adultery and now God exposed it. David's reaction to the confrontation was to admit his sin to men and God.

If you're quick to admit you're wrong, you'll be quick to become strong.

Integrity isn't the state of sinlessness, but it is the place of honesty with God about our sin.

David truly repented for his sin. He kept his integrity and had no concern about his reputation.

Since the beginning of creation, mankind has struggled with integrity. Adam blames his wife when confronted by God. Eve blames the serpent for her sin. Yes, they sinned. But they complicated matters even worse by trying to cover up their actions in the face of our all-knowing God. No integrity. No honesty.

I believe that God is so excited to see someone being honest and open with him, that he rushes into that person's life to enjoy their integrity.

Job lost everything but his integrity. He eventually got twice as much than he lost by keeping his integrity. Don't fall into the trap of the self-preservation of your public image. Instead fight to develop and maintain your personal integrity with God, yourself, and others. God finds such a person irresistible in a world engulfed by self-promotion and self-preservation.

People's opinions of you can and will change frequently in your life. But God's opinion of you is constant and unchanging. Integrity is proof to God of your trust in Him. That trust will not go unnoticed or unrewarded by God.

CHAPTER 6

The Nightmare at Our Dream House

I don't know why, but I stubbornly clung to the desperate hope that Mary and I wouldn't be forced to file for personal bankruptcy. Of course, this proved to be impossible. In every lawsuit, Mary and I were included along with the church. When we lost access to the insurance companies' unlimited resources, we quickly exhausted our own and were compelled into filing for personal bankruptcy.

Several years before all this had begun, the church board voted unanimously to transfer the church parsonage, where our family lived, into our names. My associate pastor was tasked with that action. Mary, myself and the board all assumed it had been accomplished. But it hadn't. For whatever reason, he didn't follow through with it, even while assuring us he had. The moment the church had filed for bankruptcy, we lost legal control of our house.

One day, several years before this, my beautiful young daughter, Melody Joy, asked me if we would ever have a house of our own. At that time we were renting and the house we lived in needed major repairs (kitchen ceiling falling in, backyard fence falling down, etc.), but the landlord wouldn't do them.

I told Melody what God had told me as we pioneered, "If you build My house, I'll build yours." I told Melody to draw a picture of the house she'd like Jesus to give us. She came back with a very cute and colorful drawing of a two-story house with a pool. We put her picture on our refrigerator and would slap it and say, "Thank you, Jesus, for our miracle house" every time we walked through the kitchen. In just four months, God gave us that house!

We found it one day when Mary and I were just driving around the neighborhood in Scottsdale where our church had been for 5 years. We saw a beautiful two-story house for sale and stopped to briefly look at it. I lifted Mary up so she would see over the fence into the backyard where there was not only a large pool, but a sand volleyball court, horseshoe pit, fire pit, children's playground and garden area.

She said to me, "This would be my dream house, but I know we could never afford it."

Well, it ended up being a foreclosure that the church bought for a fraction of its value, at $300,000.00. For seven years Mary and I and our four children were able to live and enjoy our 'miracle' house. It was a perfect place for our children and God had wondrously kept His promise to me that, "If you build My house, I'll build yours."

In my wildest conjecture and speculations I couldn't ever imagine having to leave a house that God had so supernaturally given us. But we hadn't filed the paperwork, and we were going to lose the house. It was a valuable corporate asset that now was under the control of the bankruptcy court. For several years, we made double payments on its mortgage, which reduced it to under $100,000.00. In those seven years, the house we were able to purchase for $300,000.00 was now worth $1,300,000.00. Year by year, as I watched its value incredibly increase, I always thought of it being God's provision for our retirement after the kids were grown and we retired from pastoral ministry we could sell it and live comfortably in our latter years. When we lost it, we didn't just lose a house, we lost a million dollars in equity and our future financial security. It all just vanished suddenly like a vapor of smoke.

During the week of Christmas 1998, our family was suddenly homeless. A member of the church and a dear friend, Rich DeJacimo, was able to give us a month's stay at a small hotel that had owed him financially. We "celebrated" Christmas huddled around a foot tall Christmas tree in our tiny hotel room. The juxtaposition of going from a 4,500 square foot house on one acre of land in north Scottsdale to a tiny hotel room was almost impossible for us to fathom.

Once again, I had committed tremendous effort and energy desperately trying to find a way to keep the house. I thought that was what my wonderful wife wanted, needed and would be devastated without, but I was wrong about Mary. She handled this relentless onslaught of bad news with grace, dignity and godliness. I was the one who was falling apart.

For 6 months we lived at a kind church member's house before they leased us a very nice home in Scottsdale. In our wilderness, God continued to provide for us in unusual ways and through unexpected people. As our family moved around, so did the church. Between 1995 and 2002 our church moved 22 times, from schools to hotels, to parks, to an airplane hangar. We were "the church on the move," constantly changing our location.

I put my life on hold and felt as if I was simply just going through the motions. I found out that when your life is controlled by circumstances, our happiness never lasts. If we're waiting for something or someone to change to make us happy then we are slaves to our circumstantial conditions. Our contentment and happiness must not be based upon us getting what we think we need, but our true joy as God's children comes from the power of God's kingdom within us. God's presence is joy and his presence is always with us!

The discovery that true happiness isn't the result of having all your goals met, or all your dreams realized, but instead it is God's kingdom brought to us in the person of Jesus Christ, that has the power to bring joy to anyone, anywhere, at any time.

YOU CAN HAVE ABSOLUTELY NOTHING AND STILL BE HAPPY OR YOU CAN HAVE EVERYTHING AND STILL BE UNHAPPY.

If our happiness is always based upon things going the way we want them to, or people doing the things we want them to, then we have become the emotional slaves of the uncontrollable circumstantial fluctuations of life. Something will always separate us from personal happiness and fulfillment. As long as we look for external conditions to try to bring us internal contentment we haven't yet discovered the true source of personal fulfillment and joy.

When our lives have been continually immersed in the love and acceptance of God, when we can see and feel about ourselves the way God does, then joy is the natural by-product. As we experience the ups and downs of life we are anchored by the personal foundation of knowing who we are as the children of God. It doesn't matter then if we are up or if we are down, who we really are isn't determined or even influenced by those external circumstances. We don't find our identity or meaning by either perceived successes or failures. Our successes don't make us a success and our failures don't make us a failure. We stay balanced against the potential abuses of our success and against the potential destructive impact of our defeats by the strength of our inner identity. That inner picture of who we are is not based on any of these external conditions, instead it is the image of who God has said we are.

I've counseled so many beautiful people who saw themselves as ugly and worthless. Maybe because of the harshness of their upbringing, they've never been able to develop a healthy self-image. Others I've tried to help had some kind of cataclysmic event in their life such as a divorce, bankruptcy or rape that altered their esteem and image. We are all different in how we've both experienced life and then responded to those experiences. But no matter what the experience was or how we reacted to it, we ultimately face the same reality: That we are all in need of God's healing and help to develop our true self-image.

Success and failure are revelations. Both in the mountaintops and in the valley of our lives we reveal who we are as people. When a person only experiences mountain tops of successes, the true nature of their character is never completely revealed. Yes, in the potential excesses of success, weakness is many times uncovered. In reality, though, it is in the valleys of life where we truly come face to face with who we are as people. It is the test of fire that determines the strength and quality of something or someone.

Who we really are is not measured by what we have or don't have, what we may or may not do. Those actions and circumstances have no real bearing on how God sees us, and therefore should not impact how we then see ourselves. On the other hand, when we truly know who we are as the children of God, then that reality will have a powerful effect on the decisions we make and the actions we take in life.

During this period of time, the church "grew" from over 4,000 active attending members to 140 dedicated souls who stood with us through thick and thin in those stormy years. These remarkable people represent one of the primary reasons I couldn't leave this church or this city. They stood with us in our hour of trial and tribulation, and I felt a sincere obligation to continue to serve them as long as they wanted me to.

In 1996, I decided to continue my graduate work. Over the next three years I worked feverishly to finish my masters and doctorate degrees in Christian psychology. And here's the first thing I learned: From every possible instrument of the measurement for emotional and mental health, I was suffering with a serious case of manic depression. I lay on my own counseling couch and said, "You're sick, buddy." For two years I experienced a powerfully debilitating, severe and even suicidal depression. I would sleep for 10 or 12 hours every night. It seemed like sleep was the only place I wasn't tormented and could find rest. It was an incredible experience to advance in my knowledge of education and be able to see in my own life a classic case of depression. The good benefit was the ability to locate and understand that I had a problem and what exactly the problem was. The bad thing was the same as the good thing: coming to terms and admitting to myself how sick I had become. At times, I lived totally housebound. Although I've never drank alcohol or used drugs, I self-medicated by eating my way to over 300 pounds.

Depression is like living in a very dark room where all the lights are off and the curtains closed so that no rays of light come in. It's a horrible prison and vicious taskmaster.

People with depression are suffering in every possible way. It's an emotional death sentence that has destroyed many lives and was now beginning to destroy mine.

Depression is a very difficult experience to describe in words. As a minister I supposed I should never admit to actually experiencing it personally, but such an announcement would be untrue. With my ministry and reputation both suddenly and violently torn apart, I fell into the inner emotional darkness that is known as depression. It began for me when the visions and plans that I was once confidently assured were God's will were abruptly cut off and removed from my life. When I lost hope I found hopelessness creates depression.

Depression is an inner wound that inflicts constant pain to its victim. It is an inner darkness that sees no ray of hope. Depression is an emotional prison that holds captive the thoughts and feelings of its prisoners. There is not an up side to depression. It has no lessons to teach or benefits to receive.

Depression is suffering.

Depression is destructive.

Depression is dangerous.

Anyone can be depressed. Most of us have experienced some kind of personal encounter with depression. Our emotional reaction to loss, rejection, or some other personal crises can trigger a season of despair. Most people gradually recover from such an episode and go on with their life. I believe, though, that some people are more vulnerable to fall into frequent or longer-lasting depressions than others. I know now that I'm one of those.

There are people, millions of people all around us that every day face the hopelessness, anxiety, and suffering that living with depression brings. It doesn't take a recognizable circumstantial crises to produce depression. Depression isn't the product of external pressures, instead depression is an internal condition that can be triggered by almost any circumstance.

You may be looking at people all around you who you couldn't imagine would have any reason to be depressed. That is where we make the mistake of understanding how depression works. It is the product of an inner emotional crisis that may or may not have any outward indicators or causes.

Some people face great personal loss and crisis and in spite of the magnitude of their external pressures, they never even experience personal depression. Most people have battled with depression as a result of some hardship or crisis that they have experienced. By the grace of God and enough time they were able to come through it. But there are great amounts of people that have fallen victims to depression and they're not able to climb out of the deep pit of its despair.

When you live in the continuous grip of depression, every day becomes a chore. It's hard work to do normal every day living when you are carrying the constant burden that depression brings. Depressed people are not happy people. They may have moments of happiness, but those moments are always eventually smothered by the overwhelming unhappiness that is depression. A depressed person begins to view the world and their relationship to the world in a distorted way. The longer the depression lasts, the greater their distortion of reality becomes. Everything and everyone seem to contribute to their depression.

People in this condition will do almost anything to try to escape it. They try drugs—either prescribed by a professional therapist or obtained illegally. They try with alcohol to drink away their inner pain. They try many other experiences that they hope will change the way they feel. They look for comfort in people, food, sex, entertainment, etc. The sad reality is that though they may find a temporary relief from their suffering, soon after the movie is over, or the meals done, or the effect of the drug has lifted, they're worse off than before.

The external symptoms of depression will vary with each individual person. Some eat too much, others will eat too little or not at all. Some sleep too much; others sleep too little. Most depressed people will eventually withdraw from their relationships with others. Many times they feel unable to cope with the many burdens that are a part of interpersonal relationships.

Depressed people are vulnerable. Just as a physical disease will weaken our physical bodies and make us more vulnerable to other diseases and physical conditions, depression weakens the soul and makes us susceptible to conditions and temptations that a healthy soul will normally overcome. For example, a person who has never been given to self-destructive, suicidal thoughts, may find that during a prolonged depression these thoughts are plenteous and powerful and sometimes irresistible. A depressed person often will seek to place the responsibility of his or her happiness or unhappiness (the answer to or the cause of their depression) on their relationships or circumstances. Accordingly, then, he or she may make sudden and often dramatic changes in these areas in their search for a solution. (Quitting their job, divorcing their spouse, having an affair, moving to another city, etc.)

In the Christian world, far too often we trivialize the condition of depression by throwing a scripture at somebody and telling them to "get over it," or by saying a twenty second prayer with someone and then telling them, "It's gone now." It seems especially in Charismatic and Pentecostal circles we want nothing to do with the complex reality of depression. The easiest and perhaps most ignorant reaction that many Christians, especially ministers, have to deal with in a depressed individual is to immediately place all the blame and responsibility of that condition on the devil. We want to cast out the devil of depression because that's far more simple and effortless way to deal with them than to help someone progressively walk out of depression's influence.

I do believe that if the depressed person cannot find a way to stop the downward progression of their condition, that at some point it will become invaded and infused with demonic powers. At this very dangerous level of depression, a person's will becomes overpowered by the combination of their weakened emotional condition and the supernatural powers of demonic beings. This person can be set free by the power of the name of Jesus. Any and all demons can be bound and cast out. But that is never the full extent of their freedom.

Their souls must be healed and restored from the effects and also the causes that brought about their depression. To focus solely on Satan as the total cause and controller of depression is not only spiritually naïve, it is also extremely dangerous. Any extended and uncontrolled sin or weakness will eventually attract the attention of demonic involvement. It is the fallen condition of our flesh that generates our sinful condition. It is uncontrolled sinful behavior that then will generate demonic influence in our lives.

If we are seeking to help those suffering with depression we must realize that both of these factors may be at work. There may well be demonic powers at work in a depressed person. But before demonic influence came there was something broken in their soul that preceded and then hastened the influence of the demonic. It is a lot easier to bind the devil than to deal with a broken person.

Every day we experience hundreds of different ideas and thoughts that pass in and out of our mind. Everyone experiences positive and negative, good and bad, and godly and evil thoughts, every day. The difference in a chronically depressed person is that their thought's process tends to be almost entirely negative. Depression creates a climate where positive, healthy and godly thoughts are prevented from entry, or if they do enter, from abiding in the mind and emotions of the depressed.

This negative mental climate is by its very nature, an enemy of the depressed individual's freedom. They view themselves negatively. They view the world and their relationship to the world negatively. The depressed person doesn't think positive, healthy thoughts because they can't. So theirs is a vicious cycle of more and more negative thoughts and attitudes about life. Every perceived failure and rejection is magnified much greater than its actuality in their soul. Even small experiences become much more significant and harmful to the depressed person than the reality of the circumstance. The impact of the normal everyday give and take of life becomes a perilous and often paranoid daily burden to the depressed.

CHAPTER 7

When Hope Walks Out, Depression Walks In

In the autopsy of my own depression, I discovered that the day I stopped dreaming, the day that hope died in me, was the same day that depression found a home in me. When hope walked out, depression walked in. Proverbs 13:12 says:

> "Hope deferred makes the heart sick, but
> when the desire comes, it is a tree of life."

Hope is when we believe the future will be better than today. It means having an expectation for good for our future. I literally thought, and came to believe, that there could be no way for me to ever get back everything I had lost. I believed that my best days were all behind me, that the future would never even come close to expressing what I had seen God do in the past. I tried to imagine every possible future outcome and scenario and came to the very wrong, but very real to me, conclusion that the bad and evil I had been through and was continuing to go through could never become a good thing.

How can bad things ever become good? I saw no possible redemptive value in the tragic things that had happened and in so many people, including myself, who had experienced so much devastation, ruin, trauma and pain.

It creates an internal struggle, a cognitive dissonance when we are experiencing death, disease, or devastation and read in the scriptures Romans 8:28:

> "And we know that all things work together for good to those who love God, those who are the called according to His purpose."

Our minds look at the circumstances and experiences that look permanent, but God says they're only temporary.

We look at what is glaringly, intrinsically bad or evil and it seems like an impossibility to even contemplate how something good can emerge out of something evil. But God said it was true, so our true struggle is not with the possibility of evil becoming good, because God's word plainly and powerfully says that God is both able and eager to do so.

I've always had a tendency to be harsh and overly critical of my life. Now, predisposed to this self-sabotage practice, I had more negative ammunition to use against myself than ever before. Feeling constant shame for my very public failure (the worst thing that can happen to a church is to have a 'scandal,' and we had a doozy of one!) I quickly discovered that shame was feeding and fueling the depression. Because I had based most of my self-worth on the perceptions I had of other people's approval and respect, when I realized that I'd lost much of that necessary affirmation, my life fell apart. I was left with the hideous condition of shame. I was covered with the feelings of failure and rejection. But what really brought about this overwhelming burden of shame? I felt afraid to leave my house to go to a public place where people might recognize me. (Kind of hard to be a pastor with that problem!) I had never simply given myself the grace to "make mistakes," but held myself to an ultimately, unattainable standard. The problem with being a perfectionist is that you never get 'there' and therefore are never truly happy. I had to learn to accept, forgive and love myself the same way God accepts, forgives and loves me. This was hard to do, but essential to not only overcoming shame and self-sabotage, but to be able to grow into a more mature revelation of my true identity as God helped me.

More and more I began to realize that the shame I felt was not the result of changing public opinion. I knew it wasn't the result of something I'd done to grieve God. (That feeling is called conviction, and conviction doesn't destroy our lives as shame does. It, instead, leads us to repentance that brings restoration in our relationship with God.) I had slowly come to the startling realization that my feeling of shame was simply the result of the way I saw myself. I HATED WHO I WAS. Shame was the result of how I now saw myself. I hated whom I perceived I had become as a person.

It is an endless struggle of self-inflicted wounds to live with self-hatred. My sense of worth as a person was based upon my perception of people's acceptance. The mirror that I used to obtain my self-worth and image was suddenly shattered. I had fallen into a trap of dependency that had then transformed my heart into an internal prison cell of shame.

It was now so clear to me that I didn't like who I was. All along I had used the camouflage of other people's attention and approval to validate my life.

As I now looked at my life in the naked reality of who I was as a person, I realized I didn't like what I saw. My real problem was not what the media or people said about me, it was what my own heart said about me. I was a grown man that somehow had never truly learned to like himself, let alone love himself.

Shame and rejection and self-hatred will always be the eventuality of such a condition. It's only a matter of time till they are welcomed into such a heart.

How could I hold my head up with my own heart bent over with shame? With God's help I needed to change my self-image from negative to positive. If God loves me and if He unconditionally accepts me then I must learn to love and accept myself. If God calls me valuable, then I must look at myself as someone who has been given value and worth by God.

MY VALUE AND WORTH DOESN'T COME BY SUCCESS OR ACHIEVEMENTS BUT BY MY RELATIONSHIP TO GOD.

GOD GIVES ME VALUE SIMPLY BECAUSE I AM HIS CHILD.

I had to introduce my shame to God's love. When I did, and as I continue to, his love chases away the dark shadows of shame from every corner of my heart. God's love is making a brand new man out of me. I believe the things I do in life (husband, father, pastor, etc.) will all be affected by who I'm becoming as a man.

As we know, and then experience, God's love, we experience internal change with every encounter love has with us.

When we can see ourselves with the eyes of God, then our own self-image and worth will begin to grow and develop properly. The Bible is the Revelation of God's thoughts to you and me. As we personalize the precious promises of God spoken to us in the scriptures, seeing and saying the same things God sees and says about us, we build a healthy inner life, developing the image God has given us as His children.

Most of us have some understanding of the fact that God loves us. We hear it, read it, sing it, and say we believe it. But did you know that if every friend you have turns their back on you, if your family angrily disowns you, if public opinion suddenly turned against you, that in spite of all those circumstances, God will never stop loving you. He will never leave you. He will never give up on you.

It's one thing to believe God loves you, it's an entirely different matter to experience God's amazing love first hand. To be loved by God is to be changed by the power of this love. At the core of all of our lives must be this simple yet profound truth: I am the child of a loving heavenly father, and it is His love, acceptance and grace that fill my life with value, worth, and purpose.

We are all the children of God. It is the voice of our natural fathers that shaped so much of what we became as children. But for all mankind it is the voice of our Heavenly Father what will build our spiritual identity into a firm reality. It is in the loving hands of our creator that we experience His love and find true fulfillment.

Real spiritual warfare is not what's happening to us, but rather what's happening inside us. The enemy's most strategic, aggressive and continuous assault against our lives will always be an attempt to deceive, confuse, distort and destroy our identity as the children of God. When we are governed by the presence of rejection, condemnation, shame and depression, they are ultimately the evidence that we've not yet embraced our true identity in the Kingdom as the children of God. My depression was evidence of an internal battle in my soul for control of my self-image.

Our real battle is coming to the place that we can trust God and believe His word over our lives in spite of all contrary circumstantial evidence.

For believers, hope is not an exercise of positive thinking based on human reasoning and supposition. Christian hope is always based on our loving God and in His unfailing promises to us in the scriptures. Our hope needs no natural evidence or confirmation, only the promises of God to us and the Spirit of God in us. We were made by the glorious design of God to flourish under the presence and influence of hope. As the scripture said, "But when desire comes it is a tree of life."

When we dream, we give birth to desires, desires from God for our future. These desires are a "tree of life" to our inner life, our soul and spirit. As we feast on the future by rehearsing these dreams, desires and hopes, we give fuel to the core of our very being.

Hope is heaven's medicine for our soul and it can carry us through the most difficult and devastating moments of our lives as we hold to it and believe in it. It's impossible to be a happy person as long as we have and hold to a negative outlook concerning the future. Hopelessness is always a part and parcel of depression, and beginning to dream, desire and hope is always a part and parcel of overcoming depression.

I remember the day years ago when my son, Tim, who at that time was about 3 years old, and I were sitting on the couch watching TV. A commercial for the DeVry Institute came on.

At the end of this advertisement for their school, they show a student who looks into the camera and says, "My future's looking great!' The next thing I know, my three-year-old son looks over at me and says, "Daddy, my future's looking great!"

Something in me as a father leaped for joy hearing that from my young son. I can only imagine how our heavenly Father must feel when we rightfully believe the same about our lives as His children - that the best is yet come.

I decided one Sunday to tell the church the truth about my horrific personal battle with depression. Up to then, for 20 years of ministry, I had always been able to distinguish and separate my personal life from my public ministry. Even in the two years of a debilitating depression, when it was time to teach, preach and pray, I would shift gears and fulfill my ministerial obligations. But almost immediately afterwards I would find myself subject to the influence of depression over my live. But that Sunday I decided to do something different: tell the church the truth about my life. It wasn't that I was lying to them before this, only that I chose to withhold personal information.

"Church, for the past two years I've been suffering from a severe, manic depression."

The silence that filled the auditorium was palpable, but I noticed something immediately after the words left my lips. I started feeling better! So for the next several weeks and months I practiced what I like to call "honesty therapy." When I couldn't wait for the next service to share more about my life, I was reminded of the man in scriptures with a withered hand. Jesus told him "stretch our your hand," and the moment he did, his hand was healed. **If we reveal it, God will heal it!**

The church gradually became used to this ministry philosophy. Now we are a church that practices "honesty therapy": and people feel safe to be themselves and reveal their real hurts, pains and issues.

During this same time I was watching Christian television when an awesome, black pastor from Dallas came on. His name was TD Jakes, and the more I listened to him, the more it spoke deeply to me. Shortly thereafter, I got on a plane, flew to Dallas, Texas, rented a car and drove to The Potter's House Church. I walked into their, church bookstore and met a woman at the bookstore. I said to her, "I want a copy of every tape you have of Pastor Jake's preaching."

She looked at me funny and probably thought, "This is one crazy white person." Walking into the back room I could hear her talking to others. After some time she reemerged with almost 75 different cassettes of Pastor Jakes. As I paid for them, she put them into a brown grocery bag and sent me off. I went right back home and began to listen to those tapes every day. I experienced what I had taught: God's Word has the greatest healing properties of anything on this planet.

Only a few weeks before this, one evening at the dinner table with my family, I looked into the beautiful faces of my four blue and green eyed, blond-haired children and I noticed something I'd never seen before. They were all beginning to become sad. My depression had now become my children's sadness.

This was unimaginable to me to think that my life was so dramatically and negatively affecting their lives. A light went on that day on the inside of me. Right there I decided to do whatever it would take to get better. I refused to be the reason my children would need to go to therapy as adults, trying to get over and recover from the consequences of living with a depressed father.

Our children were then, and still are now, everything to Mary and I. And they're all the motivation I needed to begin the journey to recovery.

Human beings are created in the image of Almighty God. We were designed to do more than just endure and suffer in this life. God gave us the ability and the creativity to dream.

It is the dreams of our forefathers that created this great country called America.

It is the imagination and creativity of men and women throughout history that has helped solve so many horrible problems with inspired ideas and inventions.

This ability to see past our present into our tomorrow comes from God. He is the God of hope. In every nation where the Gospel of Christ has been shared and received those nations have become prosperous, creative, and inventive. Everything about the Gospel is infused with hope. Every promise of God's word is an arbiter of hope. God's promises produce hope in the heart of the believer. Prayer is by its very nature a hope creating and hope confirming experience. We ask because God has promised to give. We seek because God has promised to reveal. We knock because God has promised to open. Perhaps the greatest singular hope that God offers us is the promise of eternal life. The hope of eternity with God. In the big picture of our lives, it is understanding that we will share eternity with our God and His children in heaven.

This hope then becomes the anchor of our lives as Christians.

For true hope to be successful it must be God-based and God-inspired. Our hope must be built upon and then rest in God. God is hope. God gives hope. God created us as His children to live in hope. The human experience deprived of hope, descends mankind into the abyss of darkness and despair. At any age, in any place, under any circumstances when hope is removed from a person's soul, depression and its destructive counterparts will enter without resistance to work as much havoc and destruction as possible. But when hope comes to the hopeless it is like a ray of light into a darkened room. The more hope becomes a reality, the brighter and brighter the light and the lesser and lesser the darkness in our soul.

Many times we are surrounded by situations that seemingly offer us no signs of hope. Bad times come upon the righteous and the unrighteous, both Christians and non-Christians alike. By nature, personality, and experience, some may find it easier to be hopeful than others. But regardless if it's easy or if it is hard, hope is the doorway out of the prison of depression.

When our situation seems hopeless, we must build our hope in God and His promises unto us. The closer we move towards God, the greater the hope we receive from His presence and promises. It is an amazing human reality that so many times when we face an injustice or crisis in our lives, that one of our first instinctive reactions is to think it came from God. The quicker we conquer such a falsehood, the quicker we can recover with God's help. God is not our enemy, He's our friend. He is not against, us, He is for us.

Picture a large castle that has been made from giant stones and is surrounded by a large mote. This castle was built from the ground up, stone by stone. Finally finished, it has become a giant fortress against all enemies. That is what depression is like. Depression is a fortress of negativity and despair. Each negative thought and attitude become a stone that builds it higher and stronger until it becomes a powerful stronghold. Inside this castle there are no windows or doors, no candles or lights, only pure darkness. The prisoners of this fortress are under the unrelenting intimidation and anxiety that depression's darkness produces.

The way to destroy this stronghold is the same way you built it. One stone at a time. One thought at a time. One day at a time. Hope breaks the castle's walls wide open and allows the light to come into the castle. Hope by its nature is positive. It is the thoughts and promises from God that lift, illuminate, liberate, encourage, inspire, deliver, and heal. These God-inspired positive thoughts and words are the very essence of what true hope is.

The Bible describes this process in 11 Cor. 10:3-5:

> "For though we walk in the flesh, we do not was after the flesh. For the weapons of our warfare are not carnal, but mighty through God to the pulling down of strongholds. Casting down imaginations and every high thing that exalteth itself against the knowledge of God, and bringing into captivity every thought to the obedience of Christ."

A stronghold is a house built by thoughts and inhabited by darkness. Hope is a divine weapon against the stronghold of depression. In every area of our life when hopelessness has tried to bring depression, we can conquer this foe by tearing down its castle of thoughts and attitudes, with the power of hope. No matter how difficult your life's reality may seem today, no matter how painfully or disappointing your life was yesterday, you can and must have hope for your tomorrow. Hope is healthy, joyous, inspiring, motivating, and encouraging.

WHERE THERE IS NO VISION THE PEOPLE PERISH...(Prov. 29:18)

Vision is essentially the attitudes, dreams, and plans you have about tomorrow. Vision is always about the future because we can see our present and remember our past but we must dream about tomorrow. Vision is a house of hope built by the promises of God's word and the dreams God gives us. If we perish without a vision then the opposite must also hold true, our lives will flourish with a vision.

Creation and everything in it are the manifestation of God's vision. We are the product of God's vision. Your tomorrow will be the product of your vision today. That's how important vision is. When Jesus ascended on high, the Bible says that He sent the Holy Spirit, the divine comforter back to earth. As the Bible goes on in detail to describe the nature of the ongoing work of the Holy Spirit from that time until today, we see a picture of the purpose of His work among us.

"And it shall come to pass in the last days, saith God, I will pour out of my Spirit upon all flesh and your sons and your daughters shall prophesy, and your young men shall see visions, and your old men shall dream dreams:

> And on my servants and on my handmaidens I will pour out in those days of my Spirit; and they shall prophesy."
> (Acts 2:17, 18)

The three manifestations that this passage of scripture gives us concerning the work of the Holy Spirit are:

- Prophesy
- Visions
- Dreams

All three are the promise of God to give us revelation about our future and destiny as His children. Prophesy, vision and dreams are three different spiritual tools that all share the same spiritual purpose: To give us a vision, hope and dream for tomorrow.

The Holy Spirit by His nature and function is a depression destroyer. Because God knows the limitations of our flesh and the continuing battle we face with hopelessness, at the very forefront of the Holy Spirit's mandate and function on earth, was the solution to depression in vision, dreams, and prophecy. Through these divine instruments the Holy Spirit can liberate any life from the control of depression. In every area of our life, in any season of our life, you can receive destiny, purpose, and vision through the person and power of the Holy. Spirit. That doesn't mean your battle with depression will be easy or quick, but it does mean that we have the tools in God's word and Spirit to wage a winning war against depression.

There is no fear in love; but perfect love casts out fear, because fear involves torment. But he who fears has not been made perfect in love. (I John 4:18)

It's astounding how many problem areas of are lives come back to the same genesis; a lack of love at some vital stage of our lives, the inability to receive God's love and the inability to love ourselves as God does. The list could go on but you see my point, so many issues and problems in our lives surround our individual experience with love. Depression is an inner anxiety and anger about how we feel life has treated us. It is impossible to deal with those inner anxieties and complexities without addressing the love issue. We need to be loved to be healthy individuals. We never grow away from the need to be loved. Jesus only gave us two commandments. He summed up the entire law and prophets—hundreds of individual ordinance's—hundreds of thousands of civil regulations and laws in this statement in Mark 12:30-31:

> "And thou shalt love the Lord your God with all thy heart, and all thy soul, and with all thy mind, and with all thy strength: this is the first commandment."
> And the second is like, namely this, "Thou shalt love thy neighbor as thyself. There is none other commandment greater than these."

Jesus makes it clear here that love is the priority of the Christian life. The fact that we are commanded to love God as well as each other suggests to us that God desires for us to realize the tremendous value of love. It is impossible to have any kind of personal experience with God where we express our love towards Him, without in each and every encounter also being the object of God's love back to us. God is love and in His presence and by His promise we are touched and transformed by His love.

When we experience God's love, either by a personal encounter with Him, or by an experience with an individual filled with God's love, our lives are impacted and enriched.

God's love heals hurting people. Christ's commandment to love was much more than just another law to keep man from sinning. This commandment gives us a true key to understanding our needs as human beings. We need to be loved and we need to give love.

In relationships with others where we can both give and receive love we will be emotionally and spiritually healthier by our continuing exposure to love. Our healing and health as human beings is dependent on our relationship to God and then to people.

This "relationship principle" is at the very core of the Kingdom of God. Jesus continuously taught us about the attitudes and actions that make healthy, godly relationships. We must understand the great effect love can have on an individual. We must also then prepare ourselves to love others by being filled with God's love and then positioning ourselves to love others by reaching out to those around us. When people are hurting we must reach out to them and not be so easy to give up on them. When we see someone beginning to withdraw from relationships and trying to isolate themselves, instead of letting them go, we must make every effort to love them back into health.

Inside of CFTN during worship.

Worship Nation worshiping during
service during at CFTN.

Outside overview of Church for the Nations

Maiden Family

Pastor Mike speaking at Church for the Nations

CHAPTER 8

The Unbelievable Power
Of The "F" Word

One day I heard the still small voice of the Lord in my heart say, "Would you like to be healed of all the hurt and pain you're experiencing?"

I immediately responded with, "Yes, Lord!"

What He said next to me was both surprising and intimidating. He said, "Then I want you to forgive and pray for everyone who has hurt you."

At that time, every day I would drive our two oldest children, Melody and Matthew, to their high school about forty minutes away. While driving them there and back, I'd make four trips on the same road every day. On this road was a church that represented great hurt and pain in my life. A few months before, when things were only beginning to erupt and it looked as if the church could withstand the storm, our associate pastor and his wife, who were also our dearest friends and closest confidants, had decided they'd had enough of all the craziness that was happening. They proceeded to contact four hundred families, which included all the top givers and church leaders. The wife was our book-keeper and could easily access the church giving records and contact the families. They had a "secret" meeting where our associate pastor invited all those leaders and givers to join him in leaving our church and joining a church mile away.

When they all left, we were so shocked and hurt that our best friends had originated and organized it all. The church they all went to doubled in size overnight and promptly began a building program to handle their new "growth." Driving past that property four times a day was not the most pleasant experience, but Mary and I decided when we were first married to walk in love and not speak against people, preachers, churches or anyone. So instead of saying something inappropriate about that church, every day I would just slightly turn my head or look far down the road so as to not look directly at it.

Yet I had a major problem now: God has called my attention to this and the many other situations and people and was offering me a remedy from the hurt and trauma if I would only forgive, pray for and bless them all.

Ouch!

I know too much of the scriptures to disagree with God about the command we've all been given to forgive, so no need to attempt to make my case against doing so. So I just told Him the truth, "I'll do it Lord, but I won't mean it because my emotions feel something quite different than love and forgiveness for them."

"Just do it," He said.

And then I had the most illuminating mental vision. I saw a train that went on very long. It had an engine at the front, dozens, perhaps hundreds of cargo cars and finally at the very end a caboose. Across the outside of the engine was written in large letters the word "FAITH" and at the very end across the caboose was the word "FEELINGS." I saw that the Lord was telling me to initiate my "FAITH" by forgiveness and blessing to the people who'd hurt me and that the reward I'd eventually receive would be that my feelings would follow and align with my faith.

Every day for the next 5 or 6 weeks, 4 times a day I would stretch out my hands toward that church and declare my forgiveness and God's blessings towards them. By faith, every day, yet nothing of consequence seemed to be happening in my emotions. I still felt what I had been feeling.

Until one day, during this prayerful exercise of faith, everything changed. As I prayed for them, I felt an ocean of love and compassion for them. I realized they left because they were confused and hurting and things weren't getting better in our church. I understood that all that church's pastor did was receive broken and bruised sheep that needed a shepherd and a place to feed and be healed.

Most strikingly, I became completely aware that I wasn't hurting anymore. All the hurt, pain and trauma had all left, just like the Lord promised me it would if I'd forgive and bless them.

It's hard to be happy when you're hurting. It's hard to overcome depression while you're still hurting. It's very hard to heal others without being whole ourselves. Everything in my life changed on the day when He took my pain away.

Who is being hurt by bitterness? When we refuse to forgive others for hurting us, who is affected by our choice? Unforgiveness hurts you. When we choose not to forgive someone, we are only further punishing ourselves. Anger and bitterness are the malignant children of unforgiveness. When we choose not to forgive (that's what unforgiveness is), we never allow closure and healing to the hurt in our own lives. The hurt lives on in our anger and bitterness. Our unforgiveness becomes the prison cell of reliving yesterday's hurt over and over.

Somehow our mind tells us that it is a normal and even healthy reaction to our own hurt to raise up the defenses of bitterness and anger. Surely if someone else was in our shoes and had experienced the same hardships, then they would also share in the same emotional responses. We use this rational to justify our continuing anger and cynicism towards others. But what if that kind of reaction was not healthy or good for us, that even though it may be a normal human response it can be very destructive?

Our minds may tell us that we're getting back at those that hurt us by our anger or that this kind of emotion is healthy, but it's not good for us, nor is it healthy. As we trace the poisoned flow of our anger upstream, back to the source, there we will find the unresolved hurts and disappointments of our life. Each unresolved hurt contributing to a greater manifestation of anger and bitterness in our life. In many people's lives the river of resentment and anger grows larger with every passing year, until suddenly it is visible to all and unable to be controlled or hidden anymore. Instead of infrequent explosions of our temper, we grow more and more are angry all the time. Our bitterness becomes such a part of our life that we're permanently cynical about people and life.

No matter what kind of poison runs through the river of our life (anger, bitterness, resentment, cynicism, hatred, prejudice, violence, abuse, etc.), the healing solution must always include forgiveness. Through forgiveness we release our hurts and those who have hurt us from our lives and place them both into the hands of God. There God can heal all our hurts and deal with those who have hurt us. The act of forgiveness is an act of love. It is an act of healing. God's love naturally responds to being hurt by forgiving. God forgives us because He is love. God gives us the gift of His love so we can have the power to forgive.

Broken relationships create broken hearts, but through the act of forgiveness the healing process starts.

God's real big on forgiveness. He basically tells us not to bother to ask Him anything in prayer if we have unforgiveness in our hearts. Our unforgiveness nullifies our prayer and our faith. The way God looks at it, He has forgiven all of mankind for all of their sins. What a massive work of grace that truly is. Sin is no longer the deciding issue in our eternal destiny. Only one thing lets us into God's heaven or sends us into Satan's hell: do we personally believe that Jesus Christ is the son of God and that He died to forgive our sins. When we say yes, we receive what He's already done. When we say no we reject this free gift of eternal life. So the fact is that our sin has been once and for all washed away by the blood of Jesus Christ. So in God's eyes, our sin is forgiven. Because of His wondrous gift of undeserved but total forgiveness, God commands us to forgive one another, all the time, of everything. The scope of our forgiveness cannot be compared to God's forgiveness to us. In those relative terms, because we've been forgiven much, we must forgive much.

Forgiveness is more than just a means to personal protection and well-being. Forgiveness is a spiritual force. When your heart lets someone out of the prison of unforgiveness, you are allowing a new and greater level of God's involvement in your life. When a young godly boy named Stephen was falsely accused and even murdered by being hit with rocks before he died, he opened his mouth and professed his forgiveness to his murderers. Leading the pack of religious zealots against Stephen was a Pharisee name Saul. Saul is almost immediately visited by God in a supernatural fashion and is called to be an apostle. The forgiveness of Stephen was responsible for the salvation of Saul, who later became Paul who would pen two-thirds of the New Testament.

Through the conflicts that I was thrust into, forgiveness has become a necessary and vital part of my recovery. At first it seemed doubly hard for me to practice forgiveness in my situation. It was in my role as God's servant, doing what I thought was God's will, that my life and reputation were assaulted. I was offended and was sure that God was offended for me. But ultimately such thinking is just camouflaged self-righteousness. At first I assumed my indignation was born of a righteous nature, but that wasn't evidently the case. So, in the ever exciting world of church splits, lawsuits, and scandals, I have learned that to overcome I must forgive. Forgiveness wasn't optional for my restoration, it was always the first and most vital step to be taken. So now when I drive by several churches that are almost entirely made up of my former church members, I stretch out my hand and ask for God's blessing upon the people and pastor.

It is always a crucial mistake to wait until you feel forgiveness towards someone before you act. If you wait until your heart assures you it's now feeling able to forgive, you will wait too long. Forgiveness is an act of your will, regardless of your feelings. Forgiveness sets in motion the love of God, both in the person we've forgive and in our heart that's been wounded. Forgiveness sets into motion the healing power of God's love. We often tell people that we love them, but when we forgive someone, we show them that we love them.

Forgiveness is the face of love. Without forgiveness there would be no salvation, no redemption, no possible relationships between God and man. There is no Christianity without its foundation stone of forgiveness. When we choose to forgive each other, we are manifesting God's love in front of an unforgiving world. While He was still hanging on the cross, in the agony of an all day long torture by Roman soldiers, Jesus lifted up his voice and prayed for the forgiveness of his accusers and executors. Because He forgave us then, God forgives us now. Forgiveness is a greater force than hatred, or strife, or any other powerful negative emotion. Forgiveness may seem weak to many but in reality it towers over all as love's great conquering champion. Forgiveness never loses the battle that it's brought in to. When you forgive, you win, period. Forgiveness has the power to undo years of hurt and misunderstanding. It has the ability to push back the powers or darkness and to free us from the far-reaching spiritual effects of the sins of our forefathers. Forgiveness has the power to heal nations.

There may come a day in your life when you are caught off guard by an unexpected broken relationship or hurt. Maybe up to then it was always fairly easy for you to forgive others. You know you're supposed to do as you are commanded by Christ, but this time it's different. This time it's personal. It's your integrity and reputation that's been wounded. Maybe the hurt was personally violent to you, in any sense it might be someone who was very close to you who has now offended you. The intensity of your pain and reaction is stronger than ever before. What would you do if such a day were to visit you? You'd do what you know is right, forgive those who have hurt you. You'd do this knowing two important things. Number one. This scenario is a pitfall trying to snare you into an offense through unforgiveness. It's a spiritual trap, set up by your spiritual enemy. This is an attempt to destroy your influence as a child of God. If you fall into the trap and stay there, you lose.

Secondly, this is an opportunity. This mostly unwanted opportunity is possibly far more important than we can see at the time. Far beyond it's violent impact and influence on our life, there is something in the destiny of God's purpose for you about to become a reality. There is promotion if we pass this test. Our opportunity has come disguised as a gruesome offense, that has brought with it real pain and suffering. But nevertheless it is in these moments of crisis that we best find out who God is and who we are. It is there that champions are made and destinies are received. It is there that we stand at the crossroads of life with our future depending upon our actions. In the bloody battlefield of today's godless world, it is forgiveness, the champion of love, who will be left standing after all others fall.

There is literally no pain, hurt or trauma you're carrying that our loving God can't heal you from, just like He healed me. I have a ministry now for hurting people based on my own story and testimony. What Satan designed for evil, God has turned for good. The same thing can and will happen in your life as you, by an act of faith, forgive, pray for and bless those who have wounded you in any way. It will change your life!

I quickly began to do the same thing with every person I felt had hurt me and found out the words of Jesus are so true: "Blessed are they who mourn, for they shall be comforted." (Matt. 5)

As God's children, living in the power and life of His glorious kingdom, we have unrestricted access to initiate a healing season and process into our lives anytime we choose to by the action of forgiveness. Don't allow the pain of your past the right to rob you of what today could be and what tomorrow holds.

NEVER GIVE THE TEMPORARY PERMISSION TO BECOME PERMANENT.

It's a lie that your heart can't be healed by God's love and grace.

It's a lie that your best days are behind you and not in front of you.

It's a lie that your wound is so deep and its pain so strong that nothing can touch and heal it.

It's always a lie to believe that we can't change, that things won't change. "Weeping may endure for a night, but joy comes in the morning." (Psalm 30:5)

God's incredible grace is more than up to the task of tackling and overcoming any and all of our life's needs and struggles.

At one point, I received a federal subpoena that required my testimony in the sentencing phase of Hank's trial. Just as my lawyers had said he would, Hank and his legal team delayed his trial for as long as it was humanly possible. And on the very first day of the trial he changed his plea to guilty, thus ending the verdict portion of the process and leaving only the sentencing portion to be done. I walked into the federal courthouse and made my way towards the court-room. There, I was directed into a large conference room to wait my turn to testify.

As soon as I entered the room, someone sitting at the far end of the conference table began to uncontrollably weep with their head down on the table. I was startled and unsure of what was happening - if this person was in a medical emer-gency. So I quickly made my way to her and realized, walking toward her, that she was actually saying something over and over while uncontrollably crying with her head down. In a sobbing voice, I finally could make sense of her words.

She was repeatedly saying, "Can you ever forgive me? Can you ever forgive me?"

For the moment, I was completely unaware of who this was. I gently placed my hand on her shoulder. She finally looked up at me. I realized that, yes, I did know her. She and her husband were members at Eagle's Nest, who had lost $1,000,000 in the Ponzi scheme. It was their lawyer who called the church and demanded a million dollars from us or else he would go to the press.

We didn't and he did.

The front-page headline of the Scottsdale Tribune read, "Pastor Advises Couple to Invest $1,000,000." They led with that bold headline and it was a complete and total lie. When this couple moved from the Midwest to Scottsdale and became members of our church, they requested a meeting with me. In this meeting they said that the wife had received a large inheritance, and they had decided together to invest the entirety of their money in one of his companies.

My response was that "they shouldn't put all their eggs in once basket" and should take their time, seek other financial experts opinions before acting. Upon hearing my advice, the wife became angry, agitated and verbally scolded me for "not supporting a businessman in your church." My advice was to not invest with him. What was screamed across the front-page headlines was the exact opposite.

Now, here I was, talking with the woman who had smeared the church and me in the paper with a grotesque lie. She looked up at me in true agony, with mascara running down her face, her eyes flooded with tears that had spilled onto the table.

Without even needing to prepare the right words or process what this moment meant to both of us, I said, while holding her in my arms, "Please don't cry for me. I forgave you long ago and I've been healed of all the pain."

I proceeded to pray and encourage her and let her know I was ok and she would be ok, too. I felt nothing but compassion and care for her, because the Lord had healed my heart of all the pain from the past.

Only God could do that!

But I'm not somehow a unique, isolated or even unusual case. What God did and continues to do for me, He'll do for anybody - including you! He's the healer of broken lives, hearts and homes and He's ready to show you what He can do. Take the first step and forgive everyone of everything! Not just because it's the "right thing," but because it's the very thing that will bring healing and wholeness into your life!

In the Bible, God used a powerful, young man named Joseph to rescue his family and prevent an entire generation from dying of starvation. But before he became a great and godly leader, he went through years of betrayal and false accusation that culminated in an unwarranted and unjust prison sentence. The hands that betrayed Joseph didn't belong to strangers or enemies, but were the very hands of his own older brothers. The men who should have been his mentors and examples were, in fact, his betrayers and enemies. They were engulfed with jealousy, envy and rage, seeing their father's great love and favor lavished on the young Joseph, but mostly absent from their own lives.

Their father, Jacob, loved Joseph's mother, Rachel, but not the other sons' mothers. They were children born into a duty-bound, but unloving relationship in a very dysfunctional home environment. Unable to contain their anger and envy, they stripped Joseph of his "coat of many colors" an sold him as a slave to traveling merchants, who proceeded to take him to Egypt. Then he was sold once again to a high level Egyptian government figure named Potiphar.

In spite of the injustices and violence, of his transportation to a new country and a radically dichotomous environment—from beloved son to a powerless slave—Joseph prospered working as a slave at Potiphar's house. His prosperity was the result of the dreams God had given him as a young man that he would be the leader and patriarch of his family someday. He lived with the internal temperance and character of a Prince and a Son, even though he was seen by all others as nothing more than a pauper slave.

The VISION we have for the FUTURE determines how we live TODAY.

In another, almost unbelievable turn of events, Potiphar's young wife was attracted to Joseph and continually sought to create an adulterous affair with him: After his consistent rebuffs of her persistent advances, she finally became enraged and falsely accuses Joseph of attempting to rape her. Guess where this future great leader, world-shaker and history-maker ends up next? A jealous husband throws him into prison. Joseph is given a "life sentence" and in spite of another horrific betrayal, the Bible says that God was with Joseph and "gave him favor and made him to prosper in the prison."

Joseph spends several years in prison until he is abruptly released one day by the command of Pharaoh and the authority of his palace guards. His season of injustice was about to end and the destiny he was born for, that he had often dreamt of, was now, after 13 long years of struggle and suffering, about to be to be released. His time finally come:

> "Pharaoh sent and called Joseph, and they
> brought him quickly out of the dungeon;
> and he shaved, changed his clothing, and
> came to Pharaoh." (Genesis 41:14)

Joseph literally 'ran' from the prison to the palace. There was both urgency and acceleration required in his transition from the 'wrong' place to the 'right' place; from 'man's' place to God's place; from his 'enemies' to his destiny. God is able to "Restore the years to you." (Joel 2: He's able to give you, in ten weeks, what you've lost and been waiting for ten years. God is able to 'accelerate' the normal cycles and rhythms of life and do so very much in a brief period of time.

The palace guards handed to Joseph a razor with the instructions to shave off his prison beard. It would be vitally important for Joseph to not look like a slave/prisoner when he stood before Pharaoh. His future didn't really care about his past. He would be of no value, unable to access and then succeed in the promise of his destiny as long as he looked like and was controlled by his history. He had to shave it all off his face. His identity and self-image had to match the tremendous promise of his destiny, not the trials of his history. He had to 'be' a prince, not a prisoner, to fulfill his heavenly purpose. So he shaved off thirteen years of disappointment, injustice and suffering.

The last requirement of Joseph was to "change his clothing" before he could access his divine calling. The palace guards handed him an ornate, beautiful, princely garment and asked him to put it on. Not over his prison clothes, but instead of them. This was not Joseph's first time he'd changed garments. His own brothers had angrily and violently 'stripped' Joseph of his coat of many colors when they betrayed and abandoned him for twenty pieces of silver. That was his first stripping.

When Mrs. Potiphar made her failed, last and most aggressive attempt to seduce Joseph, he ran away from her and left his garment in her hands. She would use it as false evidence showed to her husband to unjustly convict him of a sexual assault.

Twice before, Joseph had been 'stripped' by others: His brothers by betrayal and Potiphar's wife by false accusation. Only this time he was not being unwillingly and unjustly 'stripped' by others. This time Joseph was asked to change his own garments. He gazed at the glorious, new wardrobe that had been delivered to him and then looked back down at his own old, familiar, worn thin, dirty and worthless prison clothes. He had to make a choice. He had to first 'take off" the old garments before he could 'put on' the new. The new was not an addition and incorporation of the old, it was a personal and permanent replacement for it. He had to 'let go' of the past before he could 'get hold' of the future.

Suddenly, supernaturally, but not surprisingly (he had dreamed of this his whole life), Joseph becomes the Prime Minister of Egypt, the second most important and influential person in the greatest empire in the world at that time. His 'gift' made a way for him and delivered a generation from starvation while building immeasurable wealth for Pharaoh.

Joseph called the name his firstborn son, Manasseh: "For God has made me forget all my toil and all my father's house.' Then, he named his second son Ephraim: "For God has caused me to be fruitful in the land of my affliction."

The name of Joseph's first son, Manasseh, means "to forget." God had graced Joseph to 'forget' all the anguish, pain and betrayal of his own family. He was free of the wound and trauma they had poured out on him.

Here's what the Lord said to me as I began my journey out of the bitter pain I was controlled and consumed with: "When you choose to forgive those who have hurt you, I'll anoint you to forget the pain they've caused you."

I've had my 'Manasseh.' I've experienced the glorious grace of God that has "made me forget" all my pain and brokenness. In my mind I will have the memory of those events, but the pain and power they held over me has all be "forgotten." It doesn't hurt to remember them because the suffering and pain that once as attached to the memory is all gone! Manasseh!

Joseph used the word "toil" to describe the unwanted and unhealthy legacy his family had left him with. The Hebrew word for toil means, "Sorrow, labor, grief, pain, exhaustion, trouble, misery, fatigue, anguish, to labor to the point of exhaustion."

If any of these words give a description of what you've been feeling and experiencing, then it's time for you to have a Manasseh season when you choose to forgive and God anoints you to forget.

In the New Testament, forgiveness is at the very core, at the very center of our Christian faith. God has unilaterally and unconditionally forgiven us of all our sin and, as His children, commanded us to walk and live in a life governed by the practice of forgiving others all the time for everything.

The main Greek word used in the New Testament for 'forgive' is *apheiemi*, which means "to let go." When we forgive others, we let go of the offense, anger, bitterness, hurt and pain we feel. When we don't forgive, we the 'hold on' to all that has happened along with all the negative emotional consequences they brought.! The person who forgives will always be free, able to forget whatever and whoever because of the tremendous power God has deposited in the act of forgiveness.

Whatever you've been through, whoever has done hurt to you, it's time to LET IT GO, so you can be free, forget the pain and become fruitful in God's purpose for your life. Just like Joseph, we all have a choice whether or not we're willing to let go of the pain of the past and put on the promise of the future. The beautiful garments of a new life are being held out to us to take and put on if we'll first take off all the 'stuff' from our past by forgiveness.

I'm sure you've heard this popular saying before, "Time heals all wounds." I don't believe that's true. In fact, I believe that when we ignore and refuse to deal with our 'issues' and hurts, that they not only don't get better, they grow worse. Anything left to itself gets worse. Your untreated and unhealed issues eventually pollute every part of your life - your physical health, your relationships with others and God, your emotional well-being, and everything else.

A woman in the Bible had an issue of blood and because it wasn't healed, it "grew worse" and even cost her all her finances. Time can only be a healer when we invite Jesus into our issues by revealing them, forgiving others and receiving God's healing love and grace through His word and Spirit. Here's the truth for our lives: Jesus heals all wounds!

CHAPTER 9

The Uncertainty Principle

When these unwanted, hurtful and destructive things began to unfurl in August of 1995, I made an internal declaration based on an inaccurate estimation of my personal capacities and endurance. I decided and declared that, "I can handle about six weeks of this." It took seven years, not six weeks, for things to finally change for the good. I had no idea at the beginning how long the storms would endure and I certainly had absolutely no idea that I could last that long myself.

After losing all our church properties, we moved into Chaparral High School in Scottsdale for our Sunday morning services. This was after meeting in a huge tent for a year on the church property where our new building wasn't finished. One Sunday, a dear friend and great man of God, Dick Mills, was ministering while we were still in the tent. His message was titled "The Perfect Storm," and while he was speaking, a freakish wind, unheard of in Scottsdale, of forty to fifty miles per hour, started pounding the tent. Although we had the assurances of the tent's qualification to handle up to seventy-five miles per hour winds, let me tell you, it was very unpleasant and quite scary to watch huge speakers and light fixtures sway back and forth while Dick Mills spoke. It seemed to be a perfect metaphor for my life and church: the perfect storm: part God, part men, part Satan.

After moving to the high school, a nice woman reached out to Mary and I to help us. We were feeling shell-shocked by what had and was happening and her apparent concern for us meant much. She lived in a mansion in Scottsdale and at one time even opened her home for our family to stay when we became homeless. Her name was "Samantha" and we were convinced God had sent her to stand and support us in our time of difficulty and struggle.

One day Samantha met with Mary and I and told us that she wanted to buy us a church building. She directed us to find and assign a real estate agent to begin to look for a property that she would pay for. Her children drove Ferraris, she lived in a mansion and said she was a Harvard educated lawyer practicing international law. It all looked good to us— we were way too depleted and exhausted to delve into a more thorough examination of her life. We had lived in her house, seen her love and faith and trusted everything else was as it appeared to be as she had said.

We found a closed car dealership on a busy road in Phoenix that had a large showroom. In just a couple of weeks Samantha gave us the keys to the building and said it was ours debt free! We remodeled the showroom and started having our services there.

The church started to grow again and we were very grateful to have a home and a new beginning. After being in the building five months, on Easter Sunday of 1999, we arrived early to prepare for what we fully expected to be a glorious Resurrection Day, only to find the doors padlocked and the property guarded by private armed security and a Maricopa

County sheriffs deputy. I frantically asked what was going on - how and why had they taken possession of our 'debt free' building? They gave me a phone number of a banking executive who proceeded to inform us that they had not received any payment on that property from Samantha and were exercising their legal right to reclaim what was theirs. They confiscated everything inside the building as well.

They hadn't received a penny, but we were told it had been completely paid for. I think we met in a park that sad Resurrection Sunday. For the next year we met in different hotels and meeting halls, sometimes given only a day or two notice on not being able to meet. We were the church on the move, again, a tiny group of dedicated lovers of God, moving around the city from place to place like unwanted nomads. We finally ended up in an airplane hangar next to the Scottsdale airport.

Samantha also ended up in federal prison for stealing millions of dollars from 'investors' over the years. She pled guilty. Just like Hank, I believe Samantha had a very genuine faith in Christ. They were both born again children of God, but like many Christians they had temptations and weaknesses that they were not able to overcome. In their business lives, they strayed from the path of honesty and integrity and fell victim to greed and the shortcuts of dishonesty deception, lies and deceit to obtain wealth.

Do I believe they're Christians? Absolutely.

Do I believe they behaved in very unchristian and ungodly ways? Absolutely!

It seems incredible that during this season of almost regular uncertainty, I became almost used to it. I realize now that the Lord was healing and strengthening me. I realized that His incredible grace was always enough for whatever challenge I faced. Like Moses declared, "As your days, so shall your strength be." (Deuteronomy 33 :25(b)) To completely trust God even when nothing makes any sense is the key to surviving seasons of uncertainty. I was learning to trust God like I had never before. I was almost completely powerless to "make things happen." Things were happening and I was learning to adjust to the 'new normal' and go with the flow. I felt like my old friend, Job, who said, "Though He slay me, yet will I trust Him." (Job 13:15(a)) We trust God when we believe, even while we're enduring hardships, difficulties or other 'bad' things, that He's able, somehow, someday, to make them become "good' things.

It was about this time, things really hit home. All of my sons and daughters are awesome young men and women that any father would be more than proud to call his own. I'm both overwhelmed and humbled by the beauty, gifted-ness, strength and godliness of all four of our incredible children. For that I give God (and their wonderful mother) the complete credit and glory. Being a preacher's kid is a pretty unique and intense experience. Even in good circumstances, where there isn't the unfathomable hostilities of public scandal, or such, being a P.K. is difficult, demanding and many times unfair. If being a P.K. is hard in the best of times, it is unbearable in the worst of times. That all my children today are great people, loving spouses and parents and passionate followers of Jesus is quite a miracle, considering all they've endured.

Perhaps even greater, is the unbelievable strength and grace my beloved wife, Mary, has privately and publicly displayed our whole marriage long. Mary was able to maintain a sense of normalcy for our children when our lives and circumstances were anything but normal. We have always put family and children before vocation and ministry and that went a long way to bringing some balance into their young lives as we endured tremendously difficult circumstances. My wife is the real hero of our home. I wonder how many other women could have endured what she has and still stay in their marriage, give everything to their children and serve selflessly in the church? I'm so grateful that, as a young man, I refused to play the "dating game," but asked and waited till God brought the right woman into my life to be my wife. I couldn't have picked someone back then by myself that would fit me now. I'm so thankful for my beautiful, virtuous and godly wife, Mary.

But even with all of that, we still faced a challenge.

Matthew was a phenomenally gifted athlete and star player. Can you imagine losing all your friends in one day? Matthew was a young teenager when things fell apart at church and his world was rocked by the consequences. We didn't discover it for a couple years, but Matthew started using drugs around thirteen years old. He hid it well at the beginning, still being a star athlete and an excellent student. Around 16, we discovered and immediately intervened with personal counseling, drug therapy and tons of prayer. He was self-medicating from all the pain that had descended into his world. From 16-18, Matthew not only didn't stop doing drugs, but escalated from marijuana to cocaine and other more serious drugs.

He moved out of the house at eighteen. For the next year and a half he ran wild on the streets of Scottsdale. We did everything we could to maintain a relationship and contact with him. Drug dealers tried to kill him, the police wanted to arrest him and we just wanted our beautiful son back.

I thought it was hard to lose a church, but when we lost our son it was the deepest pain we'd ever felt. Mary and I would sometimes go into his former bedroom, lay in his bed and cry over our 'lost' son.

One day, just after his 20th birthday, I felt the Lord say to me to "Stop mourning for your son. Start thanking Me and talking to him as if he's already delivered from drugs and restored to his calling and destiny."

I told Mary that we needed to stop talking about where he's been or where he is now, but to "call things that are not as though they were." From then on, when we would see Matthew, we'd talk to him as if nothing was wrong in his life. He's always been a kind and polite gentleman, so even when his eyes were bloodshot, he'd look at us like we were the ones on drugs when we talked to him about destiny and God as if nothing was wrong.

Within weeks of doing this, a friend of Matthew's from his college basketball team invited him to a special service they were having at their small church. Matthew said, "Yes," and went. That night our mighty and loving God delivered my beloved son from seven years of drug addiction! He moved back in with us as a transformed man! Soon afterwards Matthew attended the honor academy at Teen Mania for a year and then went on a long missions ministry to Haiti. After coming home from Haiti, Matthew became our youth pastor at church.

One night, while attending his younger brother's high school basketball game, he met Candice, who would become his future wife. They have three (so far!) beautiful children.

It broke my heart that the trials and storms of my life found a way into my son's life and hurt him. It was so incredibly painful to have no alternative but to "turn him over to God" when he was bound by drugs and not ready for help or freedom. But there's no greater joy in life than watching God deliver, heal and restore one of your children who's been bound and suffering! My son is a mighty man of God today. He's an awesome husband and father and successful business-man. My son is our trophy of God's goodness and grace. If God could do this for my son and our family, He can do it for your children and family. The God of the comeback has restored our family and He is able and willing to do the same for yours. Don't give up on anyone in your family - God won't. It's not too late for them or you. It's time for your family's comeback!

CHAPTER 10

The Bitterness Of Betrayal

I had always felt about the church the way a husband feels about his wife. My commitment and my love for those people and families were very strong. I felt protective of the precious souls that made up our church family. Because of my commitments to the church and my personal struggle with rejection, I viewed any action of harm against the church or myself as its pastor, as an act of betrayal. I'd never really experienced the poison of personal betrayal until the shaking of the church.

I was so disappointed and overwhelmed by the behavior of many of my leaders. I had entrusted them with visible and vital leadership positions in the church and they had rewarded me by stealing people's money, building their own ministry and even trying to take over control of the church. There is nothing as bitter as having your friends become your enemies.

It is an inevitable reality, that in this life people are going to let you down. It is a further inevitability that you will more than likely experience some form of personal betrayal during your life. We see all around our valueless society the ruins of betrayal in broken marriages, families, businesses and churches. So no matter how good you feel about trusting someone, or how good you feel that you know somehow, someone is going to hurt or even betray you.

OK, now that we know that, or maybe and unfortunately have endured that, what do we do now? I know Jesus said to love our enemies, forgiving and blessing them, but he couldn't have possibly been talking about someone who betrayed us, could he? Yes, he was. Jesus made remarkable champions out of men who were moral traitors just when he needed them most. (Peter and Paul, for example)

Being hurt or betrayed by someone else is not enjoyable to endure. But betrayal can tell us something about our own hearts. Many people feel betrayed in life by a general feeling of injustice, that life itself has betrayed them with disappointments and tragedy. Others feel a sense of betrayal by institutions they trusted, governments, churches, hospitals, corporations: somewhere in the dealing with one of these institutions, they were hurt and betrayed. Others have had a relational breach and betrayal between themselves and someone they once loved and trusted.

The general theme in most betrayals is that our expectation of someone else's feelings and behavior have not been met. To one degree or another they have disappointed our expectations of them. Some purposely and intentionally, others maybe by misunderstanding or lack of communication. Regardless of who or how, we must now deal with the consequences of feeling betrayed.

When we put our trust in institutions, circumstances or people, then we are destined to be disappointed to some degree by their actions. We must place our trust continually in our God who will never betray or disappoint us. Then when people hurt us by disappointment or betrayal, our life is not shattered, because we may love them and have a measure of trust in them, but all of our trust remains with God.

If someone fails me, God won't.

If someone hurts me, God won't.

We cannot expect to find in people what is only found in God. So when people disappoint us and don't meet our expectations, we are protected from becoming the casualty of bitterness and cynicism because our true confidence and faith is in God alone not in men and women.

No one will ever experience the degree and quality of betrayal that God has endured. Beginning with Adam and continuing in us today how can God deal with the perpetual failure of man? Every time we choose sin over obedience; every time we reject His still small voice; every time we rebel against His word, we betray Him.

But in spite of all this massive evidence against us, Gods love for us remains steadfast, unmovable, and unconditional. The only man who ever lived his entire life without betraying God in sin was Jesus Christ. The reward that we offered the sin-less son of God was to crucify him. So it's safe to say that God is now familiar with the pain of betrayal. Yet it is the awesome power of His love that dominates who God is and what He does. It is the unrelenting nature and expression of that love to mankind that frees us from the penalty of our own rebellion against God. The multitude of our sin is no match compared to the magnitude of Gods love. Love wins, love will always win.

So then the answer becomes clear to us and the children of God. We are to follow the example that God has set for us. We are to love as He has loved. In the person of Jesus Christ we have the model of successful living. When our lives believe in and receive Gods proven love for us by personally appropriating our salvation by the blood of Jesus, we are washed from our sin and filled with Gods love. God is love and as His children we have been filled with love. Therefore we have the capacity to love as God loves. We have the capacity to forgive as God forgives. God's love makes it possible for us to overcome the pitfalls of life.

God doesn't react in anger or disappointment to the rejection He continues to face from mankind. This love He has for us is pro-active. He loved us before we knew or loved Him. He cares for us, regardless if we care for Him. He is unshaken by who we are or in spite of what we've done.

People form relationships and associations with other people based upon mutual benefit or need. But God had nothing to benefit from His long standing relationship with man. We have nothing to offer God that He doesn't have. What meaningful gift can the creation give its creator? But God is love and it is the amazing nature of this love that motivates this relationship with man. We are the continuing object of God's love and desire.

When we see the many different realms and relational associations we will have in our lifetime. From close family members, to friends, business associates, acquaintances and others, in all these different levels of personal relationships we will experience good and bad, acceptance and rejection and everything in between. No two people are emotionally identical, as no two relationship will be identical in nature.

In our many different spheres of interpersonal relationships, there is a way to be successful and fulfilled. That way is to enter into relationships already whole and satisfied because of the love, acceptance and purpose we have found in our relationship with our Heavenly Father. If we receive this love through a right relationship with Him, then we are able to enter other relationships not looking or needing love and acceptance from them. Instead we willingly, pro-actively love and accept others before or even without their love and acceptance of us.

When we enter into relationships of any kind by putting upon those relationships certain expectations based upon our need or desires, those expectations can become weighty burdens that many times cause heartbreak. So many people have learned to live their whole lives continually reacting to negative experiences they've had with other people. For example, people have told me they are never going to attend any church every again because somewhere in their past they were hurt at a church.

Many times I've heard a man or woman tell me that they are never going to get married because of a bad experience in their past. We are so used to forming our relationships because of the hunger of our own heart for love and acceptance. But what would happen to our relationships if we were already loved and accepted by God before we entered into relationships with people? If we learned to daily receive God's love and approval how then would we behave towards others?

Would it still hurt to be rejected or betrayed? Yes, I think it will always hurt us to some measure. But would our lives begin to crumble apart because someone hurt us? No, because once our lives have become fully grounded upon the foundation of God's love, we then find our identity and value from God. Then as we enter into relationships with people, we come not seeking what we need from them, but instead giving to them what God has given to us.

There are two inevitable directions a relationship based upon need can take, First the crumbling heartbreak of broken expectations. We needed that relationship to complete us and to meet our needs. When that doesn't or no longer happens, we are wounded by the realization of our unfulfilled needs. The second direction is that when we put the pressure of our expectations upon others many times they grow physically, emotionally, or spiritually weary of what appears to them to be a one-sided relationship. They realize that what they're really being asked for, they are incapable of giving. (No man or woman can take the place or fulfill the role of God in our lives.)

Many couples enter into marriage with one or both partners, expecting to be fulfilled and made happy by their relationships. But I've found it to be true in counseling many different couples, if you're not happy (with yourself and life) before marriage, you're definitely not going to be happy afterwards. The pressures of marriage will magnify our personal unhappiness and unfulfillment. It's not fair to your spouse for you to expect them to make you happy and complete. It's not fair to any type of relationship to create such a burden of expectations. But if both marriage partners allow their lives to be built and strengthened in their personal walks with God, then out of the strength of God's love they will build a strong home.

We face what we so many times consider to be failures or disappointments in our relationships. But God's love doesn't consider it a disappointment or failure just because our actions were not reciprocated. God's love doesn't write people off or throw relationship away because someone fails or hurts us or them. God's love doesn't come to receive but to give, so there are no relationship-destroying disappointments with that kind of unconditional motivation. If we allow ourselves to receive God's love until it changes us, it will give us identity and acceptance. Then we are ready to love others no matter how they respond to us. We're then ready to live life with a pro-active strength and vision because we've already found the answer to our needs in the love of our God.

CHAPTER 11

Where has God Gone

In the Charismatic church world we truly have come to love and appreciate the tangible manifestation of God's presence in our lives and church services. This wonderful emotional ecstasy is incomparable to any other human experience. God likes us to experience Him and we love the wonders of such experiences. But what becomes of the person or church that God decides doesn't need, for whatever reason, this spiritual blessing for a season? What if God decided we were too controlled by our emotion and our need for experiences. That our simple faith is in God is enough. Have we become so dependent upon certain emotional indicators that we're ripe to be deceived by hunger for an emotional experience? What if you stopped "feeling" God's presence like you used to?

When you "feel" God you don't need faith to believe He's there. I don't need to trust that He's always with me when I can emotionally or even physically sense His presence. But when we can't feel Him does that mean He's not with us? Does the lack of the usual stimuli indicate that God has abandoned us? What do we do when we no longer "feel"

God the way we used too? Our only choice in such a circumstance is to live by faith.

By faith in God's word we know who God is and what God does. His word promises us that He'll never leave or forsake us. Even if I can't feel Him, He is always with me. Even when my emotions can't sense Him, He is still always there. I know this is true because God said it. The fact that He promised it makes it an eternal reality.

Sometimes in the midst of especially trying circumstances, we wonder if God is there. In the lion's den or fiery furnace of our tribulations our senses seem to often tell us that God's not there. How could God be in the midst of evil and destructive circumstances? There is something about our condition as human beings to believe that when things are going good, God is always there. But when things are going bad, God must not be there. Though this seems true, it is not.

We must stop drawing a straight line between our natural circumstances and our understanding of God. God is not evil because we had evil visit us. God is not bad because something bad has happened to us. We must know beyond a shadow of a doubt that:

WHEN TROUBLE COMES,
GOD DOESN'T LEAVE

God is not intimated by the intensity of our lives' trials or troubles. When we feel like He's not there, our feelings are unreliable instruments of spiritual reality.

WHEN THE FEELINGS GO,
GOD ALWAYS STAYS

I think I've never experienced the sense of isolation like the one that came upon me through these events. One day I lost my two closest friends in the ministry, as they chose not to stand with me during this crises. Friends gone, leaders gone, members gone. I was overwhelmed with the force of this sudden rejection in my life. I know that some people were confident that when they left, God would leave my life too.

And when they left, I felt as if God left too.

Our feelings are frequently very fragile and unreliable. Our feeling can tell us that everything OK in our life but the reality may be the opposite. If our lives are based upon the leadership of our emotions, we will be consistently deceived and disappointed. No matter where you are right now and no matter what you're going through, God is with you. It may feel as if He's a million miles away but He's not. He's with you for all of your life.

I like having feelings—I can get real emotional about my family and my God. I shout real loud at my kids sporting events. I get excited at church and my emotions are involved in my worship of God. Emotions are not bad, they're just not dependable. When you stop "feeling" God, it doesn't mean anything. It doesn't mean God's mad at you. It doesn't mean He's taken His hand and anointing off your life. It only means you can't feel Him. He's still there. He will still answer your prayer and speak to you heart. He still will wrap His arms of love around you. God is God when I feel Him and when I don't. God is with me when I feel Him and when I don't feel Him. God loves me when I feel Him and when I don't.

When feelings lift, our faith has the opportunity to deepen in God. When we are unable to sense Him in the adversity of our circumstances, we know by faith He is still right there. The anointing of God's presence isn't some kind of emotional experience. It is a spiritual reality that we may or may not feel. The evidence of His presence is not how many goose bumps we felt in the song service, or how many tingles we had up and down our spine. The proof of God's presence is simply the power of His promise. He said it and that's solely what our faith must be built upon, His word to us.

The feelings will probably come back. But regardless if they do, or if they don't your life is not built by feelings, it is built by faith. Faith doesn't need or even consider feelings to know the truth, faith knows that if God said it, it is eternally true.

WHY ARE YOU ANGRY?

All of my life I've never had any real problems with anger. I would get angry at certain points of my life (like we all do) but hardly ever act on it and always repent from it. But something began to happen deep inside me when these powerful events transpired in my life. I began to experience an increasing level of impatience and anger. It was like an underground river of hot lava that was increasing more and more in my heart.

I had a perfect measuring instrument for my level of anger in the opportunity to drive my two oldest children to high school for four months. The drive took about one hour each way to their school. Phoenix now has the fifth worst traffic congestion in all of America. So here in this daily ritual that would last three plus hours, it became for me an anger test.

To say I was shocked would be an understatement, when I discovered how low my patience level was and how high my anger level had grown. This pressurized environment was an amazingly accurate revelation of how anger had been building up in my heart. Although I could conceal its ugly explosion by being disciplined enough, it didn't change the reality of its growing presence in my life.

To my shock and horror, I had become an angry man.

Being a Christian and a long-term minister, I was truly astonished that something I knew it was so wrong could have crept into my heart almost totally unnoticed. I began to examine the nature of this problem I faced with prayer. Why was I angry? Who was I angry with? What caused this anger to build in my life? I had come face to face with the understanding that I had become an angry person. Maybe no one else could see it but I could. I knew it was wrong and I wanted it out of my life as soon as possible.

Because of the tremendous complexity of these circumstances, and the amount of people involved, there was no simple solution to answer the question of what or who was to blame. There had been many people, including myself with many different degrees of responsibility and accountability for what had happened. As I examined the nature of my anger, I realized that much of it wasn't directed at any one particular person, but instead was a general feeling of anger towards life. I realized I was angry at those I felt had betrayed the church. I was also angry at myself for making so many mistakes in judgment. I was even angry with God. I was angry also at what had happened to the church and myself.

It had always been relatively easy for me to discover the anger I felt towards those pastors and leaders in the church that I felt had hurt and abandoned the church. I felt like I had made much progress in this area by praying for these men fairly often. Every time I felt anger toward those ex-leaders, I would try to pray for them. I truly was making head way in overcoming the hurt and anger I felt toward them.

It was far more difficult for me to finally realize how angry I had become with myself. I had directed much of the frustration and vexation I was experiencing towards myself. I can see now how the problems with rejection and a bad self-image and self-worth, helped create the perfect environment for self-hatred and anger. I was punishing myself for my public failure by internalizing my anger. Anger was like fuel to my attitude of rejection. I couldn't seem to forgive myself for allowing so many things to go so terribly wrong. I felt I deserved to be critical and unforgiving concerning my inept leadership and decision-making.

This kind of inner anger feeds the work of depression in a person's soul. Anger was like the prison keeper over the dungeon of my depression. I had internalized all the frustrations I felt about what had happened and directed most of that unassigned anger at myself.

The last focus of my anger was definitely the hardest for me to discover as well as the most difficult to come to grips with. I was angry with God. By directing my anger at all of life and at the total experience of what had happened to me, I was indirectly directing it at God, whom I know has ultimate authority over my life. God had allowed injustice, false accusation, hurt and loss to flood into my life. I had to struggle with a real feeling of betrayal for what transpired in my life. Where was God's protection, vindication, and justice?

I normally would be afraid to ever think those kinds of thoughts about God. But now I was not only thinking them, I was feeling the powerfully bitter consequences of their continuing presence. I had preached about the goodness of our God for twenty years all over the world but now my mind couldn't grasp the understanding of how a good God could let everything get so bad in my life. I tried to ignore the intense feelings I had towards God. I was very ashamed and convicted that I could actually feel that way towards God. But I began to see clearer and clearer that I would never conquer the intensity of my anger and depression without addressing my feelings towards God.

As a part of my desperate search for real answers I turned to God's word. As I began to study and search in the word of God, I was astonished to find a new revelation and understanding that I had never truly seen before. In almost every book in the Bible in both the Old and New Testaments, there is both the historic accounts of God's chosen, beloved children suffering and also a multitude of teaching on suffering.

Somehow for many years I had paid almost no attention to such examples and teachings. I felt they would be a negative influence on people if I taught them. I also felt that I was somehow safeguarded from their presence in my life. Every leader in the Bible suffered greatly. Their suffering wasn't related to their lack of faith, "open door to the devil," personal sins, or ignorance. The suffering or persecution, false accusation, slanders, beatings, imprisonment's and even deaths were the result of their righteousness and holiness.

How could I have missed this vital spiritual principal? I think because my early roots as a young minister were in the "faith movement," some of my basic perceptions were unbalanced concerning Christianity. I do appreciate so much of what I learned in those early years by some wonderfully anointed teachers. I learned to love God's word; to understand the power of faith in God; to believe God for healing and miracles; and many other essential Christian principles.

But somehow through all those years and teaching I came to have a basic misconception that most people's suffering was directly related to their lack of faith or sinfulness. I felt that there was always a direct correlation between a person's circumstance and their behavior. In other words, there must be a logical, reasonable cause for everything that happens in our life. The problem is that it's not what the entirety of the scriptures teach us. That's not what the examples of both old and new testament saints show us.

At least as often as the Bible declares God's promise to bless His children, the Bible also continuously warns us of the suffering and affliction that is a part of all of this life and especially a part of the Christian life. The early church was not persecuted, beaten, and imprisoned because of this "open door to the devil," or because of their "lack of faith." On the contrary, it was their uncompromisingly godly and faith filled lifestyles that offended the religious world, the secular world, and satanic world. Are we better than they? Are we wiser that they were? Do we have more faith than they did? I think not. If Christ himself suffered, will we not then suffer too?

I think that in America more than any other place in the world, we connect success and achievement with our brand of Christianity and ignore the mountains of scriptural and historical evidence of the hardship and suffering that the church has endured for two thousand years.

Let's go back to my earlier stated problem. If God is good (and of course He is), then how could He allow human suffering? I believe the simple answer is that God allows human suffering because He has to. Let me try to explain.

When God finished with creation, He then gave Adam, who was created in His image, dominion and authority over His creation. He handed the keys to His creation to Adam. Adam sinned and by his sin handed the keys to Satan. God then sent his son to take the keys back from Satan and redeem man from his sin.

But that doesn't change the fact that when man sinned against God, the entire earth was plunged into the effects of his actions, the curse of sin. So the planet and the people on it today are living in a sin-corrupting, satanically-defiled, evil-infested environment. Man is responsible for creating the horrible condition of human suffering. Satan is responsible for further corrupting and perverting God's creation.

God doesn't promise to keep us from trouble, but He does promise to keep us during trouble. He never promises to stop adversity and affliction from entering our lives, but He does promise to bring us through it by His grace. We can truly experience the goodness of God even in the hard and trying places and circumstances of life. Our American lifestyle is so saturated with materialism and the drive for success. Because of that we've developed (especially in Charismatic circles) our own unique belief system about Christianity. It is basically a shallow, selfish and unscriptural picture of a God that we feel is our own private butler. Many times we act like spoiled children who are consumed by our own needs and desires. We expect life to be wonderful for us and when it's not we so easily blame God.

Satan must have really enjoyed the mess I made in my life. I was angry with myself and also with God. He (Satan) knew I could never overcome the powerful weight of that anger and depression without forgiving myself and putting my complete trust in God. I had to resolve these two basic issues in order to ever have the hope of recovery. The healing and restoration of my life required that I address, head on, the powerful emotions raging in my heart.

CHAPTER 12

Who Am I Now?

We attach significance to someone's life by what kind of value they have to our life. That is human nature. We deem as highly significant those individuals who have the gifting or influence to touch many people. We view the people around us in varying levels of their personal significance to us. We judge. We value.

The inverted working of this principle is that we can then become trapped into forming the sense of our own value as a person by the significance others give us in their lives. We then value ourselves because and to the degree others value us. This seems to work for us along as we are allowed to continually feed at the banquet of receiving significance and value from others. But living this way is always a trap. Although it appears to build value and worth into our lives, it also sets us up for the inevitable reversal of fortune, people's disapproval.

Our modern society continually builds up individuals in our culture, only then to try to tear them down. The relentless conditioning of this kind of cultural mindset has elevated the value of public perception above the worth of personal integrity. It doesn't seem to matter if we are a good person as long as we are perceived to be good. Our values have changed as a nation dramatically in this area in my lifetime alone.

There are so many tragic problems with this kind of existence, they are too many to list in one chapter. We like to think as Christians that we're different from our culture. But Christians make all kinds of superficial judgments about other believers all the time. We build up our own heroes just to watch them fall by the weight of our unbearable expectations.

We create our own Charismatic super heroes not realizing that the higher we lift them up, the further they will eventually fall. God won't have any competition for superstar standing in His kingdom. We already have our superstar, His name is Jesus Christ, and this name alone is to be exalted in the earth by God's people.

Let me give you examples of how we fall into the trap of building our lives through the perceived significance of others.

The woman in search of worth thinks she's finally found the answer to her need when she has children. The children she gives life to seem in return to give value back to her. She cares, feeds, loves, clothes and teaches her children and begins to build her life's value by how important she is to her young child. But the problem with her situation is that the older her children become, the less they are dependent on her. If her self-worth is built around her value to her children, then it will begin to diminish until the day they grow up and leave her daily influence. What does she do with the rest of her life? Where can she now derive true value and significance? How does she respond to the sudden rejection of her importance when her children are teenagers?

Our roles change in life. Our duties and responsibilities change also. If we never solve our search for significance, then we will simply attach to everyone and everything's in our life a burden they can never fully satisfy.

God alone reserves the right, and He alone has the power to give our lives the true significance and value that we need to be complete.

God people-proofs us by giving us worth and meaning. The more our value is derived from our relationship and revelation of God, the more we are protected from the trap of the world's empty promise of significance.

The businessman or woman that finds their life's significance by the value they have in their field of involvement, will find his or her life shaken if they are fired or forced to retire or face business failure of one sort or another. When your job becomes the avenue of obtaining personal well-being and self-worth, you have once again fallen into the trap of depending upon external circumstances to obtain inner-life values and worth. Many leading business and professionals have had to face set back after set back, failure after failure, discouragement after discouragement on the pathway of their journey in this world. In order to persevere and overcome the influence of powerful negative setbacks, their life, identity and security have to become based upon some other image rather than the current picture of defeat.

So many people today are afraid of taking anything they perceive as a risk in their professional and personal lives. What is the power that stifles the creative and adventurous spirit in so many lives? It is the powerful fear of failure. If we are so afraid to fail, that we never are willing to try something new and different because of that fear, our lives are robbed of so much opportunity that could have become incredible victories. So much of the substance of the fear of failure is based upon how we might be perceived by others if we fail. What will people think and say about us if we try something and it ends up in failure? Let me say something I believe to be important now.

People don't think about you nearly as much as you might think they do, and they rarely think as highly of you when things are going well for you, or as low of you when things are not going so well for you.

CHAPTER 13

Time To Take Your Life Back

From the beginning of the troubles that exploded in the church's life until several years later, I had a continuing feeling of helplessness. It was as if I was caught up in a cycle of circumstances that I had no control over. I'd pray and have the entire church pray for things to be quickly resolved but things just kept happening. We bound the devil and loosed God's will. We fasted and prayed for things to change. But in spite of all our spiritual exercises, our natural circumstances grew worse instead of better.

The cumulative effect of such an environment on me was the ongoing feeling of complete helplessness. I came to a place of total resignation that things were going to happen that I couldn't prevent. In all the previous years of my ministry I had a resiliency and optimism that had always motivated and encouraged those around me. Now the optimist in me was slowly dying due to the intensity and duration of my circumstances.

Today I look at men and women that have faced a long-term struggle of some kind and I feel great compassion for them. To face the force of unrelenting adversity day after day, month after month, year after year is a very difficult task. The continuing spiritual, emotional, and physical drain that long-term struggles extract can be great. Whether it is a personal, physical, financial, or relational adversity, many times it's not what it is but how long it endures that burdens us most. The mental and emotional toll upon those who have faced such battle's can be devastating. All around our lives are people who are just barely hanging on. Over some period of time their faith and hope have been taxed until they now feel empty and now are in jeopardy of their future.

That is why we must learn to build support systems of spiritual, emotional and physical help to such individuals. We need to become much more sensitive and understanding of these around us who've been carrying great burdens. No one should have their faith and hope destroyed simply because of a lack of relational support.

In the midst of the conflict I was engulfed in, it seemed like there were months and months that I went without receiving any good news. Every phone call was more bad news. Every new problem that we faced seemed to spawn several more difficulties that we had to endure. All the while these legal, media, and financial problems were requiring my full attention. I still had to attempt to pastor the church.

I was convinced that these fires would eventually burn out. Surely it couldn't last more than six months, or even a year. It seemed as if I had set emotional deadlines on how much more I would take. But the things did last six months, then a year, then two years, then three years. By the third year, I had exhausted all my personal resources just to try to survive. When you're in a survival mode of living, life is no longer joyous or fulfilling. Every day's new goal is to just make it through the day.

When months turned into years in these troubling events, I had learned to cope by just kind of existing. No more big dreams. Nor more grandiose visions. Almost no more hope. It seemed it was best just to ride along with these circumstances until they would finally stop. Then whenever that would happen, I would start living again. It felt like I was in a nightmare that I couldn't awaken from. My mind and emotions were submerged beneath an ocean of troubled circumstances. I knew I could start living and dreaming again whenever these things would cease.

When we put our lives on hold, because we are waiting for someone or something to finally change, we've become imprisoned by external circumstances. What if, like had happened now to me, things don't change as quickly as we thought they would? What if days drag into weeks and weeks into months and months drag into years, and still nothing has changed? What will we do then? Will we just try to survive by passing the time however we can? What happens to our lives while we wait for someone or something else to change?

Then the revelation came like a morning dawn in the darkness night: it was time for me to take control of my life back from my circumstances. I had let people and events literally capture control of my entire life. I wasn't living. I was just barely surviving. I felt like an emotional zombie who was just going through the motions of living. Why should I wait one day longer, one moment longer, being emotionally enslaved to circumstances I had, seemingly, no power over?

Somehow I had become so mentally and emotionally entangled in the events of the church, that I lost my myself. I just kept telling myself that when things would change then I would change with them. I could start dreaming and really living when this season of affliction came to an end. But that's no way for me or anyone else to live their life.

Then I made the simple decision to live again. I had no power over these staggering circumstances, but I did have the power to decide about myself. I was like a man walking out of a graveyard that had decided to finally live again.

I wasn't being fair to myself, my family, the church I pastored and the God I served by not being completely (mentally, emotionally) there for them. I had let circumstances rob me from far too much. Nothing had really changed. The battles were still enduring. The circumstances that had paralyzed my life were still standing very visible before me. The only thing that had changed was my attitude. I finally just got fed up with being a slave to my circumstances.

It reminds me of four lepers in the Bible who weren't allowed to live inside the protected city because of their contagious physical condition. Nevertheless, when the city was under the siege of the enemies attack they suffered also. The strategy against them (and the city) was to cut off their food and water supply. To slowly starve them and by the horrors of starvation force their surrender.

One day in the midst of that terrible attack the four lepers looked at each other and said, "Why sit here until we die?" They had decided to get up and live again. Well, God had miraculously driven away the enemies away and as the lepers walked into that deserted army camp they were like conquering generals. They went and told the entire city about the victory. All this happened because they had decided it was their time to take their lives back.

It was time to live again.

There are so many different reasons to stop living. There are so many ways a person can be hurt or betrayed. There is so much injustice and hardship that people face. Even though our bodies live on, our heart can become imprisoned in the pain of our past. It's time for us to come out of the graveyard of yesterdays suffering and hardship. It's time for you and I to live again.

I'd been wanting to and actually, off and on, trying to lose weight for almost ten years. It seemed though that I couldn't get back control of my physical conditions. It's hard to be happy about yourself when you are physically out of control. My weight really did bother me and I had tried to no avail just about every diet in today's market. Most people that are overweight suffer with horrible self-esteem problems. I was no different. I had resigned myself to be fat forever. My physical condition contributed even more to my lack of self-esteem and worth. Don't judge overweight people if you're not overweight yourself. Be thankful that you don't have to face the daily tortures of hating how you look and feel. Overweight people don't want to be that way. Being overweight doesn't necessarily mean you're lazy or undisciplined. Most of those who struggle with their weight are really struggling with their self-image and esteem. Food is a way many people (including and especially Christians) comfort themselves. We feel guilty about drinking or using drugs, so food becomes our means of comfort. The cycle of finding some kind of comfort this way always ends up with just continuing the depression that low and lacking self-esteem creates.

As with anything that we are controlled by or addicted to, the cycle and pattern of living this way is a real bondage that traps so many lives. I had felt trapped. But something was happening on the inside of me now. Instead of losing weight so I could feel better about myself (that is the view of most overweight individuals), I began to change from the inside out. My inner-life was going through a metamorphic change.

I was beginning to deal with the real issue of my life unlike any time before. I came to realize that my problem with food and my weight was just another connected issue about my search for acceptance. I saw that to have change in my life required that it begin and be sustained by an inner transformation. I was now ready for change in my life. Not simply because I required it in order to overcome rejection, but that I had now become empowered to change by the inner revelation and revolution I was experiencing. I didn't feel the weight of all my personal expectations resting upon my ability to lose weight. I was able to make a clear decision that wasn't based on fear or desperation. I was changing on the inside and now I had the will to change on the outside.

As of this writing I have lost over seventy plus pounds and have kept it off. I've been surprised how effortless it has seemed. I know it's not just the diet and its lifestyle change that's making it seem so easy, it is a reflection of what has been transforming on the inside of my life. Everyone around me has taken notice of the physical changes that are happening with me. I wonder if they are as aware as I am, of the dramatic inward transformation I feel is taking place.

It seems we are so conditioned to recognize and then treat the symptoms of illness and problems. But lasting physical, spiritual and emotional health requires that we find the causes of our problems. If we only address and respond to the obvious physical or emotional distress, then we are allowing only a temporary solution to a condition that most assuredly is destined to reappear. There are possibly today hundreds of successful ways to help someone physically lose weight. It is almost not even important which one you use. The real issue for us as overweight people is are we being healed on the inside? Are we learning to receive worth and value for our lives from our loving God? Can we begin to see ourselves the way God sees us? (Not the way we currently view ourselves, or the way the world around see us.) Do we truly know what it feels like to receive and experience God's unconditional love on a regular basis? Can we be happy today even though we are still overweight? Can we learn to say about ourselves the same things God says about us in His word?

We must stop waiting for the magic weight loss pill, that's going to make everybody skinny, or the magic machines or diet that will do the work for us. When we find the "why's" in our life; those unseen motivations that direct our life's actions, we can then find God's answers. God wants us to understand ourselves. We need to desire to understand ourselves. Then we need to ask God to show us who we really are, knowing that everything God reveals about us, He desires to heal in us. It's almost at the exact moment of revelation that healing begins to take place in our lives. The things that God allows us to see about ourselves have no bearing on His love and acceptance to us. But it is because of His real love for us that God reveals the areas of our heart and life that are hurting us and others.

At the same time, I graduated with a masters and doctorate in Christian psychology. When it all exploded, I had had about three and a half years of seminary and Bible school. It had always gnawed on the inside of me that I came so close to getting a degree before I went full-time into Christian service as a minister. I must have thought about doing something about it a thousand times but there always seemed to be a reason or barrier stopping me from doing anything. But when I decided to take my life back from my circumstances, suddenly I was able to take action in this area of my life that I'd been unhappy with for over twenty years. It has been like an invisible wall that kept me from making decisions and taking actions in my life, now that wall is gone. It has been removed from my life and now I can move without hindrance or intimidation.

I've shared these two personal experiences because of the tremendous impact they've had on my life. Both in the unrealized dream of their fulfillment and now in the freedom of seeing them become realities.

I know how easy and even reasonable it seems to place the accountability of our inward condition on the people who have hurt us or the circumstances that have affected us. We can look at these people and events as acts of injustice that have unwillingly made us who we are today. But to live in that condition is to be a victim. A victim of people's cruelty and circumstances control. You may have been victimized by people and events in your life, but you don't have to be a victim. You can change. Your life can be free of all the destructive influence of people and events from your past. Ultimately the power of your freedom from your past and all of its pain, people and problems, lies in your hands. It's your choice. No one can keep your heart where you don't want it to be. No one or nothing has that kind of power over you.

So if your very worst experiences and memories cannot control you unless you let them, I have a simple question for you. (It's the same question I asked myself.) Why let them? Why let a hurt from your past keep on hurting you? Why give a tragedy or crises that you've been through the power to continue to torment you? Why do we relive our failures and disappointment over and over until we're completely depressed?

You can be a victim if you want to. Someone whose entire life is controlled by the hurt, abuse, or betrayal they have suffered. Or you can take your life back from the hurt, abuse and betrayal that you've experienced. But it's a cop-out for you or I to say that we don't have any choice but to be the way we are. We are far more comfortable as people when we can put the blame and responsibility of our life on someone or something else. But no matter how good that it feels to do, and regardless of how reasonable it seems, there is just one problem with it, it's not true. When we use it as the legitimate reason for the condition of our own life, we're being dishonest with ourselves, others, and God.

Our society has fallen into the trap declaring everyone to be victims. We do this to escape our personal responsibility with the issues of our own life. It is much easier to blame someone than to take responsibility. The problem with being a victim is, you never get any better. So we are encouraged to sue people and institutions that we think have hurt us rather than face the reality of our responsibility for our actions.

But I've decided I'm not going to be anyone's or anything's victim anymore. I refuse to be imprisoned by the pain and injustice of my past. I can and have accepted responsibility for my life and I choose to live again.

CHAPTER 14

Free At Last: You Can't Hurt A Dead Man

You can't offend a dead person. Just try it sometime. Drive out to the cemetery, go to someone's grave (by the way, it doesn't matter if you knew them or not for this experiment to work) and start with the insults. That's right, let'em have it. Call them names, make faces, even threaten them if you're in the mood. I guarantee you that they don't care a wit about anything you do, because dead things don't feel any pain. If, for example and God forbid, the pall bearers at a funeral somewhere accidentally drop the casket of their dear relative or friend as they're carrying it, there's no need to open it up and issue an apology to the recently departed. When you're dead you can't be offended. Which brings me back to the events in my own life.

I have found it terribly difficult to die to certain areas of my life. I've preached for years on the spiritual principal of being crucified with Christ from Galatians 2:20:

"I am crucified with Christ, nevertheless
I live, yet not I but Christ liveth in me.
And the life I now live, I live by the faith
of the Son of God, who loved me and
gave himself for me."

I've taught and preached about denying ourselves, taking up our crosses, and losing our lives as Christ taught in the gospels. Whenever I've ministered in this area I always had the mental picture of men and women being admonished by those scriptures, to come out of the filthiness of the world and overcome the carnality of their own flesh in order to serve God. I don't think I considered that I could be included as a candidate for crucifixion. I had already given my life to the Lord by following his calling for ministry. What else could I possibly have to give up?

Well, I found out, the answer is everything. My dreams and visions, my reputation, my life. I had always pictured myself as self-sacrificing in the majority of the attitudes and motivations of my life. But when I faced the "crucifixion" (please excuse me for using such a powerful metaphor here, but that's how it felt) of different parts of life, I found out I wasn't dead in those areas by this simple revelation; it hurt like crazy. I found myself unwilling to let go of parts of many areas of my life. Even while they were dying, I'd still be looking for a way of resuscitating them back into vitality.

Have you ever done like I've done before, ask God to restore to life something He's trying to kill? It's sometimes hard to imagine why God would give us a dream just to then let it die. When something dies we see it as at its end. But God sees it at the next stage of development, ready for new life.

I look back at my life and see how insecure I've been as a public figure and minister. Whenever I would hear of someone's criticism or displeasure with me, it would affect me negatively. I wanted everyone to like me and would be shaken when I would find out everyone didn't like me. Being a minister, I've always wanted to be received and even celebrated by my peers and fellow ministers. Hearing of some other pastor's displeasure with me or the church used to have a devastating impact on me. (And there are people who feel it is their Christian duty to tell you what they heard someone else say about you.)

Perhaps you can see, as I can now, how much of an influence the well-being of my reputation had on my life's actions. Even as a pastor to people that I'm called to minister to, the ongoing fear of their rejection became a barrier to God's ministry for them. Any minister must first be the servant of God and then the servant of God's people. When the preservation of our reputation or the fear of people's rejection is a part of who we are, then we can never fully accomplish God's bidding because of our blind spots. A minister must have no thought of his reputation when he serves God's people. His heart and mind must be centered on complete obedience to God's will at any cost. The people we serve must never be allowed to manipulate what God has called us to minister to them. If we are bound by the fear of their rejection, we then lose the trust of God.

I have found a powerful freedom in the losing of my reputation. People that don't care about their own reputation are capable of almost anything. After fighting so desperately to try to save mine and after mourning so sorrowfully its eventual demise, I find myself in a new state of being. I AM FREE! I don't know exactly how to describe it except by maybe saying it's like having your greatest fears suddenly all disappear. It's like opening the curtains in a darkened room, the light chases away the shadows of darkness.

I laugh about things now that used to be important enough to bother me or even offend me. So there is truly something good to be said about being dead. I'm no longer losing sleep about building programs or problems among church members. My dreams were so big and my reputation so valued that I still occasionally battle with the sense of loss. But even while reflecting on these events brings occasional sorrow, the spiritual value and wisdom of this season of life is becoming clearer and clearer. I am so much more valuable to God dead than alive!

It's not God's job to protect my reputation and build my name. It is my job to build His name giving Him all the glory.

Jesus said, "the truth will set you free," and that is right. What He didn't say then was that only dead people can be truly free. Sure, the truth will set you free, right after it kills you.

Like with so many other areas of my walk with God, I thought I could see how God was going to do something He had promised. But God hardly ever does things the way that we would do them. So then when our way of trying to do God's will finally fails, it is God's turn to take over and do it how and when He chooses to. To be dead is this sense is to be alive to the power and purpose of God. When our life no longer interferes with His will, then His will is unhindered for its completion.

When we have the opportunity to become offended at some other person, it's not just an opportunity to possibly forgive someone for hurting us, it is also a test to see how dead we are.

You can't hurt a dead man. What inside of us becomes outraged at someone's actions or words that have hurt us? What is the basis for our indignation and anger? It always traces back to our incredibly strong instincts for self-preservation. The ultimate act against our selfish nature is to walk in the love of God, forgiving those who hurt us.

God's love is so pure and selfless. It demands that we forgive regardless of the reason or circumstances of our offense. God's love demands that we lay down our life in order to serve someone else. It is in the death of our self-preservation that we can truly unconditionally love others all the time with no calculation of the cost of that love to ourselves.

It is the businessman or woman who has had their ambition and need for recognition crucified whom God can truly use. The person whose motives have been cleansed from greed and selfishness is the person God can trust with His wisdom and wealth. That's right. God trusts dead people. So many men and women pray and seek God's abundant promise or blessings for their lives. They even tell the preacher what they will do when they have their breakthrough. Barely submerged beneath their desire for God's blessing is their hunger for recognition and fame, and their lust for material possessions.

The amazing thing about God is that when we ask for things He's promised, He's not offended because we may have hidden motivations for receiving those blessings. What God does is assure us that we can receive His blessing and then immediately begins to expose and remove areas of uncleanness in our hearts. The problem with this is that so many people think that this purity process is at odds or war with the receiving of the blessing. It's not. Many men and women refuse to remain in the place of purification long enough to be prepared to receive God's promise. But God purifies us so that the power of His received promise won't hurt or even destroy us. This process requires that we have a strong trust in God, knowing that He is the author and finisher of our faith. Also, this process results in being a measuring instrument of where and who we really are and of how desperate we are to see God's will fulfilled in our life.

CHAPTER 15

Perception? Deception? What's The Difference?

God looks at us with the awesome power of being omniscient, all-knowing. He knows every detail of our lives, past, present, and future and of the world we live in. God cannot be fooled or deceived by anyone. But you and I aren't God. We're human beings that derive most of our knowledge and understanding through our physical senses. What we see and hear creates an image of what we know and understand. Because of the limitations of receiving information this way, we are vulnerable to the ever-present possibility that things are not the way they look or seem to be. That our sense or our understanding has not discovered the true nature and reality of our circumstance.

If our life is solely governed by the understanding of our perceptions then we are invariably sentenced to be the victims of the power of deception. Smart, educated and intelligent people are captured by deception all the time. What is the weakness that led to their eventual deception? The weakness of trusting your own mind and heart to be capable of sorting out the real from the counterfeit. Deception essentially boils down to us believing something to be true that isn't, believing a lie.

The startling revelation about today's image driven, media saturated society is once we become conditioned to make our choices and decisions by our perceptions only, we then open our lives to perceptions hidden partner, deception. As deception descends upon the generation to imprison the hearts and minds of men, it has nothing to fear from the human senses and intellect. For deception knows its true nature and powers are not of a natural source. Deception is a spiritual force that can only be truly overcome by other spiritual forces.

I remember having a sort of a mental dialogue with God one day about my church. I couldn't help feeling confident by all the indicators I could see. We seemed to be so healthy as a church fellowship. The people that made up the leadership of the church seemed to be strongly committed to our vision and loyal to me as their pastor. We were growing and accomplishing much through over one hundred and fifty outreach ministries to people. Many of today's top traveling ministries wanted to minister at the church. From every possible, measurable indicator we were doing great, with what seemed like clear sailing ahead.

So with my mental state one of absolute confidence in the strength and integrity of the church, I heard the Lord tell me He was going to "visit" my church. I knew from studying the spiritual principal of visitation that when God says He's going to visit it means He's going to closely inspect and evaluate then when He visits. How could I possibly be fearful when, in my own heart I was perfectly convinced of God's eventual stamp of approval after such a visit. I remember being almost eager for such an encounter with God. I felt I already knew how things were and was excited about what I knew would be God's promotion and approval coming to the church and also to myself for doing such a good job in His kingdom.

Then came His visitation. Immediately and repetitively for a season of several months I was literally astonished to find out what had been really going on in the church. Revelation after revelation of problems with the leadership came to the surface. Elders who were con-men and thieves. Pastors who were self-promoting hirelings. Other pastors with gross moral failures. I remember my instinctive reaction to this almost overwhelming series of revelations was to immediately assume God was judging us. That had to be it because so much had gone wrong so quickly. But the longer I looked and thought about what was happening, the more I came to understand that God wasn't making these terrible things happen, instead God was exposing what was hidden in the life of the church. God hadn't made these individuals sin, God had simply exposed their hidden behavior and agendas. There it was. The true reality of what we had spent years in the building of. I was brokenhearted, sickened, and angered all at the same time. But I was no longer deceived about the true condition of the church. The revelation of the actual spiritual condition of the church then lead directly into a personal work of freedom from deception in my own life as I've written about in earlier chapters.

God loved me and the members of the church enough to put a stop to many previously hidden sins in the church. Especially relating to those in active leadership in the church. Sadly none of the exposed leaders had the courage to stay, repent, and eventually be restored. Several of them walked out of their place of leadership at our church right into another position of trust and authority in other churches.

Completely ignoring and not caring about the damage their behavior brought upon God's people. The most common reaction in these leaders to having their sin or agenda exposed was to immediately and forcefully bring accusation against me. Although not done directly to my face, it seems they wanted to inflict as much collateral damage to the church as possible in their attempt to deflect attention from their own lives. This did actually lead to massive confusion and eventual mistrust of myself in hundreds of church members.

I think an appropriate analogy to these shocking series of events would be for a husband or wife to unexpectedly be divorced by their spouse who had been seeing a secret lover for along time. To suddenly realize that something has been going on for a period of time without your knowledge, that realization brings with it a powerful emotional response. Anger, guilt, shame, disbelief, rejection, resentment, unforgiveness, bitterness, hopelessness, etc. So our inward response to being freed from deception isn't always instant joy and happiness. We sometimes feel the deepest sense of betrayal either by others or even by our own heart. But even though it can be excruciatingly painful it is always a good thing to have any form of deception exposed in our lives. God can't put His lasting blessing upon something or someone in deception. It is not in God's anger or judgment that He exposes deception in us. It is His love and care for us that refuses to let us be bound by the power of any deception.

Deception approaches our lives by offering a counterfeit, though appealing to something in us. Deception doesn't care if it finds us looking for God's will or our own will, good or bad; it will attempt to seduce our mind and heart with its counterfeit claims.

So what are we to do in this seemingly one-sided fight against such a powerful foe? We must learn to seek the guidance and wisdom of the Holy Spirit, who is the spirit of truth. God cannot be deceived and if we rely upon His help and seek His will we can and shall overcome deception.

It is so easy for us to believe that we are somehow protected by deception just because we are Christians, and because we are the children of a loving God. He wouldn't let us fall into the snare of deception.

Of course it's very true that God doesn't want anyone to be bound in deception. But it is wrong for us to imagine that because God doesn't want us deceived, we, by that fact alone are preserved from error. We must make use of every spiritual gift and truth in God's word and then bathe our lives in prayerful surrender to the Holy Spirit. Then and only then can God see us through the potential pitfalls of deceptions.

I believe that many in the body of Christ are under some form of deception: in our attitudes towards other churches and denominations; in our attitude toward a lost and dying world that Christ died for; in our attitude and motivation towards our brothers and sisters in Christ; our motivation about money. There is so much criticism and division in the church today. All these areas are just a few of the potential problems we have in our attitudes and motivations.

I wish every Christian could have the opportunity to speak to a crowd of believers some time. People will actually make faces to show their disapproval, fold their arms in disgust, refuse to open or even bring a Bible to church. We must humble ourselves if we want to be preserved from deception.

The ministry has humbled and broken me. I once was so confident and convinced that God and I could change the world. My goals are less lofty now. I just want God to change me and let that work of His spirit touch whomever He chooses.

When we face a setback of any type, whether it's the realization that we were wrong or any one of the many adversity's life can bring, we are wise to look inward and learn and grow in God's wisdom and grace. Many people live in a cycle of repeated history. They keep making the same mistakes, and doing the same things that created the environment for yesterday's problems. We can and should learn valuable lessons and wisdom from our mistakes and adversity, which in turn could help others in their time of need.

I cannot escape the reality that I'm not the same person I was before these things happened in my life. Initially I assumed that I had been changed for the worse by how bitterly and personally I seemed to experience these events. When we are consumed in the grief of crisis or tragedy, it is hard to see any hope of our test turning into a testimony. But it is the incredible faithfulness of God that endures through the faithlessness of our own hearts and lives. Now I can actually thank God for allowing me to endure these storms and adversities because He has made me a better person through them. That's something I considered impossible when they first appeared, but now my heart is overwhelmed with gratitude to God for truly "working all things together for my good."

CHAPTER 16

The Grace To Make Mistakes (or, You're Not God, So Relax)

I've always hated making mistakes, and although I've made more than my share of them, I'd usually have standards and goals that were very difficult to reach. No one would be harder on myself than I was when these goals were unrealized. I can clearly see now that it is self-defeating to live this way as it creates an atmosphere for continuous disappointment and rejection. I was "setting myself up" for even greater inward struggles by continually demanding more from myself than I could deliver.

In the singularly largest area of my life's focus and mission (the ministry and the church God called me to pursue and pastor), I was especially driven and motivated for achievement and excellence. The mental and emotional state that I lived in regarding my life and ministry, didn't prepare or equip me to face the avalanche of adversity that came pouring down on my life.

The after effects of the storms of difficulty that came upon the church left me in a numb, shock-like condition. I felt I had massively failed God. For the first time in my public ministry I had come face to face with the real limitations of my humanity. I openly wondered if God could ever use me again. I also questioned why God chose to use me in the first place. Surely He could have done much better than me in His selection for a leader and pastor.

The youthful zeal that had once driven my ministry was replaced by the startling realization of my human inability and vulnerability. During this soul-searching journey for answers, my pastor, Dr. Lawrence Kennedy came to speak to me and also at the church. His counsel to me was very simple yet very profound. After spending hours explaining every detail of our circumstances and the personal struggle in my heart and mind, Dr. Kennedy told me this, "Mike, you're not God. I've read the job description for being God and only God qualifies."

He was talking about having the grace to make mistakes. It began to set me free when I realized that God wasn't surprised or offended by my humanity and its weakness. That God was more aware than I of the intrinsic weakness of my humanity. I needed to lighten up. Heaven didn't shut down because our church had problems. God was not shocked that a group of human beings messed up. (That doesn't mean it was His perfect will or design for people to behave badly. Nor does it mean we can live in an attitude of moral compromise because "after all, we're just human.") But it does mean that: When God forgives us, we must then also forgive ourselves.

I am learning to come to terms with my humanity by realizing it's imperfection and inability and yet believing for the increasing image of Christ in my life.

We must not only have the revelation of this grace for our lives, we must also have it for others. There has only been one perfect, sinless human being that ever lived. The reward we gave Him for His sinlessness was to violently murder Him. We must learn to be gracious, forgiving, and accepting to people who fail us or God. The more perfection you demand from yourself or another just increases the level of disappointment you'll experience with your or their failure.

When Jesus warned Peter of his soon coming series of betrayals, Peter was initially shocked and offended that Christ could think so little of him. But after coming face to face with his frail humanity after the three betrayals, he remembered what Jesus said to him and wept. For Peter to ever move past that bitter failure, and in just a short time later to be the champion of the early church, meant that he had to give himself grace. He had to come to terms with his humanity or else his failures would disqualify him from ever being used of God.

God uses imperfect vessels for one very simple reason. That is all He has to choose from. Blessed is the man or woman who accepts the reality of their humanity.

As pastors we must not give people the license to sin by promoting a careless, compromising gospel. At the same time, we should not be surprised or condemning when people sin. When people sin we must seek to restore them through repentance, all the while being humble and unjudgmental knowing we share the same human conditions.

As Christians we need to have the love of God so powerfully flowing through our lives, that we learn to love our brothers and sisters in Christ unconditionally. A love that doesn't demand repayment or reciprocation. A love that doesn't throw away those who fail, disappoint, or hurt us. A love that doesn't condemn or criticize others for their human weakness. A love that helps heal the broken and restore the lost. A love that looks past the sin and sees the precious soul that Christ died for. A love that allows others to feel secure because they know you won't give up on them if they fail.

We need this love and the graciousness it produces, in the church today. There are too many wounded soldiers that have either left or been abandoned by the body of Christ. There are too many believers thinking they have failed God too severely to be a part of his church or purpose in the earth. There are too many Christians that have given up trying to live the Christian life because they feel unable to live, what they perceive, is a life of perfection.

There are too many judgmental, hypocritical churches and Christian leaders that portray themselves as better than everyone else. There are too many ministers who have created a false impression of who they really are. May God give us this grace, for ourselves, for the church, for the world.

CHAPTER 17

Sometimes There Are
No Easy Answers

When someone we know faces a crisis or tragedy, those of us who love them desperately long to be able to help them. We often search to find the right words to say hoping to be able to give them a magical healing from their pain. Far too frequently we say and take unwise words and actions out of our frustration in trying to comfort them But many times in the hardship and difficulty of life there are no easy answers. It is often best to just be there and show the hurting your love and support.

We so desire to find and know the answers to all of our questions. Modern science would rather declare our evolutionary beginnings from a gas exploding in outer space to mankind evolving from apes, rather than admit the obvious, we can't prove scientifically when and who we come from. We would rather have an answer (even if it's unmerited and unbelievable) that have to face the emptiness of not knowing. We people of faith believe God is the author of all of creation including man.

There are certain events in all of our lives that bring us into the unsettling territory of unanswered questions. We want the "whys" in our life answered by someone. We want explanations and reasoning for circumstances that bring problems or pain into our life. We find it easier to deal with hardship if we can find its cause and determine its origin. But sometimes in this life there are no easy answers or any easy solutions to unexplainable and unavoidable events we experience.

When I was younger I vividly remember listening to many "faith teachers" being very tough with poor old Job. They acted like such a book shouldn't be included in the Bible. A book that deals extensively with human suffering and human responses to suffering. The common teaching by these brothers and many others is that everything that happened to Job was his own fault. They base this explanation on only one scripture where Job said, "The thing I feared has come upon me." (Job 3:25) What they neglect to teach is that's not the whole story. Chapter one tells us of a dialogue that God and Satan are having, where God brings up Job by name to Satan. God issues a challenge of sorts concerning his faith in Job's commitment and righteousness. God then allows Satan to try Him for a season, with certain limiting restrictions on what He would allow Satan to do against Job.

There is then a fascinating study in human behavior next when Job's "comforters" try to give him counsel. One by one, chapter-by-chapter, they are determined to find the "secret sin" or "open door" in Job's life that must have led to all of his adversity and misery. Their foundational premise was that there had to be a logical explanation for everything in Job's life going so completely wrong. These four answer seekers punished Job with a series of inquisitions and accusations that only helped further Job's state of depression.

Neither Job's friends or Job himself could "make sense" out of these terrible events that shook his life. But Job ultimately passed this fiery trial for one simple reason: He put his trust in God.. Living or dead, answers or not, he never stopped believing and trusting in his God. Most scholars agree that the entire affliction of Job was well under two years in length. Job's reward for his patience and trust was to have God give him twice as much of everything he had lost. Job's life and example is one of perseverance and unwavering trust in the face or unanswerable questions and tribulations.

The folks who were dealt with in a measure of severity by the hand of God were his comforting friends. (With friends like that who needs enemies.) In their determination to place blame and responsibility with Job, they had offended God. God was offended by the terrible treatment they gave an already suffering Job. God was equally angered by the level of arrogance and presumption they demonstrated by trying to give answers that only God Himself knew. They had trespassed into God's domain and then misrepresented the word and wisdom of God in their counsel to Job.

As believers we will all face certain moments and circumstances in our life that defy logic, reason, or explanation. If God does choose to speak to us in some way to give us a measure of understanding, that's great. But what do you and I do when we can't make heads or tails of a season or circumstance in our life? Do we question the integrity and goodness of God? Do we allow the enemy to continually torment us with the "whys"? Do we seek to grasp anyone's attempt to find an explanation? The answer is no. At the end of our small solar system of understanding is the massive and unending universe of God's understanding. When we come to an end in our quest for answers, we must there and then put our complete trust in God. We must trust God even when things don't make sense. We must continue to trust Him in times of great suffering and affliction. We must trust Him in the face of injustice and betrayal.

I have recently come to greatly respect and appreciate the great faith of Job. In the face of overwhelming adversity and affliction, he refused to relinquish his abiding trust in God.

It is the understanding in the sovereignty of God that helps release a true trust in God for our lives. It is an understanding of God's ultimate authority over all of our lives as His children. He is Lord, Master, Sovereign, Almighty, Beginning and End, King of Kings. Jesus is declared as the Lord of every believer. His authority must not be questioned or doubted. In much of the body of Christ in America we don't seem to have a good understanding of the principle of Lordship. In our democratic government, we have learned to question and mistrust leaders. But a true sovereign has complete authority and power over those whom He reigns. When that sovereign is good and just the people trust and rest in under His authority. Our sovereign, the Lord Jesus Christ is perfect in every way and we must learn to put our complete trust in His authority over our lives.

I remember growing up in church when everything was a "demon." Every problem, sin, or even idiosyncrasies were assigned as demonic. I remember "coca-cola" demons being cast out and other complete foolishness. One of the causes for demon chasers to become obsessed with such silliness, is once again our strong desire to find simple solutions to every question and problem we face. We sometimes find it easier to blame the devil than to possibly not know the real answer.

We may be in a circumstance that we're unable to find even one potentially redeeming quality about. We may face the violence of something that is purely evil and destructive.

We may endure suffering and tragedy that seems so unjust and cruel. We may never fully know all the "whys" of our life. We may never come to a place of complete understanding in many areas of our lives. Each and every time we face such a circumstance, we must decide how we're going to respond to God. Can we trust Him when things go bad? Can we trust Him when we endure suffering and affliction? Can we trust Him when our healing or breakthrough doesn't happen when we thought it would?

It seems that our walk with God boils down to what degree of trust we have with Him. It is not God's duty to explain every decision and action He takes with us. Much like we, as parents, aren't required to explain the reasoning behind our decisions to our young children. We know things as adults that they simply can't know or comprehend as children. We know that is best for them much better than they know and it's not important that their little minds completely understand. They will just have to trust us as parents to do the right thing. In the same way, all of us as the children of God must settle the issue of trust between God and us. We must win the battle in our mind and heart and put our complete trust in God at all times. We must trust Him when we can see Him at work and also when we can't see Him at work. We must trust Him when we feel His presence and we're unable to feel His presence. We must trust Him when we understand what He's doing and when we don't understand what He's doing.

For the foundation of our trust in God to be strong enough to endure tough times, it must be based upon more than a selfish or shallow relationship with God. If our relationship to God is primarily based on all the good things He's done and has promised to do, then what happens to such a person when it looks like nothing good is happening in their life and it seems like God's blessings have departed?

We must be convinced of the true nature and intention of God towards us. God's nature is love and it is the revelation and experience of that love that will produce strong trust in our hearts toward Him. Unless our trust is rooted in the understanding of God's love, it will have no depth to be able to resist the circumstantial storms of life. When things just don't make any sense and life seems unjust, our confidence and trust in God will be shaken if it is shallow. When there are no easy answers and our mind is raging and questioning everything and everyone we believe in, at these points of real crisis in our lives we must have a foundation that can't be shaken. That foundation is complete, absolute trust in God. That foundation is built by the personal revelation of the love of God to us.

The Bible gives a wonderful promise about God's involvement in our lives in Romans 8:28:

> "We know that all things work together
> for good to them who love God, to those
> who are called according to His purpose."

The promise of this scripture can be so powerful and encouraging to anyone experiencing troubling times. But how many people have heard this scripture shared to them in the midst of a very trying season of their life and because they felt overwhelmed by their circumstances, forgotten or even neglected by God, they can't see any ray of hope or possibility about things working together for good. Without a deeply embedded foundation of trust, any and all such promises ring shallow and meaningless to those who are suffering. It is extremely difficult to try to build strong trust in God while you're surrounded by affliction and adversity. That would be like a construction crew trying to lay the foundation of a building while a terrible storm was raging against them. The time to lay the foundation is when the weather is not so bad! The time for you and me to build a strong foundation or trust in God is right now, before the storms come. Your faith can't keep them away, but your faith in God can carry you through it.

Being a Christian doesn't mean we are exempt from hardships and sorrows of life. Being a Christian doesn't mean that we will have all the answers to the many problems and questions of our life. But being a believer does mean that we have someone we can put our complete trust in. Someone who loves us perfectly and unconditionally. Someone who knows everything about everything and everyone. Someone who has the power and ability to handle any and all circumstances. That someone is God. It's time for us as Christians to put our trust in God.

CHAPTER 18

Beautiful Scars

When we experience truly painful circumstances and season's of our life, God always promises to be with us during such seasons and to heal us from all harmful effects it may have had on our life. God is by nature a healer. He is a Restorer and Redeemer. Every encounter we will ever have with God during our life and eternity, will bring healing unto us. Knowing He is a healer gives us real hope when we are going through suffering. Experiencing His healing power gives us great joy.

It is very important and extremely necessary for us to allow the healing process of God to begin working in our life by exposing the pain we feel to the God who heals. Unresolved areas of hurt in our lives will not just go away if we don't receive healing. They fester and grow and become spiritually and emotionally diseased with powerful negative forces if we let them. So if we allow Him, God can and will heal us of what hurts in us. He wants to. We truly need to be healed.

But what happens to us after God has touched and healed our pain? Do we completely forget what happened to us? Do we than live as if we were never affected or hurt? Do we ignore the reality of a once very painful experience? I believe that God does heal His people. I also believe that after we are healed we'll still show a scar. That scar will be a reminder to us of where we've been and what God did for us, and we as a testimony to others who may be enduring similar struggles in their life.

Some of the events and experiences I had have been so traumatic and so deeply personal that even though I have and am experiencing God's work of healing, I will never forget those experiences. I don't think God wants me to forget them either. He wants to use them to help others. He wants my scars to become testimonies of His faithfulness and grace. Beautiful scars not because of the situation or suffering being good or beautiful, but because in the painful suffering we experience a quality and depth of God's grace that truly is remarkable and beautiful. The Bible tells us in 2 Corinthians 1: 3-5 (Amplified):

Blessed [gratefully praised and adored] be the God and Father of our Lord Jesus Christ, the Father of mercies and the God of all comfort, who comforts *and* encourages us in every trouble so that we will be able to comfort *and* encourage those who are in any kind of trouble, with the comfort with which we ourselves are comforted by God. For just as Christ's sufferings are ours in abundance [as they overflow to His followers], so also our comfort [our reassurance, our encouragement, our consolation] is abundant through Christ [it is truly more than enough to endure what we must].

The awesome promise of this passage of scripture tells us of the intention and ability of God to comfort and heal us no matter what we've experienced. The knowledge that God has promised and is able to meet us and heal us in any and every possible human circumstance delivers us from fear. We don't have to be afraid of anything or anyone because of God's promise to help and heal us. He didn't promise to keep trouble from us, but He does promise to restore us.

The grace that we receive in times of affliction doesn't leave even after the affliction is over. That grace is now a permanent part of our spiritual identity. To know and understand that enables us to be sensitive and prepared to minister to others going through similar trails. To be able to see the "big picture" of the much enhanced capacity of our usefulness to the Kingdom of God, as a direct result of painful tribulations, is a tremendous spiritual and psychological tool that can bring true meaning and purpose to an otherwise meaningless, and painful experience. Sometimes that may be the only sense we can make out of troubling times in our lives.

So stop trying to hide your scars. They're beautiful in the eyes of God and they are meaningful in the eyes of men. Unless you show them, people might never know what you've been through and what God has done for you. There are no perfect people. This is an imperfect world we live in. We must realize the value and virtue of being honest and open to others about our lives. The grace that God's given you can be given to others as we open our lives and share it with them.

Most of the time in a hurting person's life they have an ability to discern the personal credibility of the individual trying to minister to them. They can tell if that other persons been in a similar struggle and condition. This ability to identify with what a person's experience and circumstances are, is a vital condition to successful ministry unto them. True, life-changing ministry is far more than just teaching and theology. Real ministry comes from the measure of God's life and grace that has been given unto us. Much of the potentially life-changing source of that grace will be what we've received from God in our own time of need and trouble. When we share this part of our life with others, it is real to us and thus it will be real to them also. We're not giving them something we heard about or someone else's revelation or testimony, instead we are pouring into them the healing life that God poured into us.

The potential of such experiences to deeply enrich our lives with God's grace are tremendous. To live every day knowing that anything and everything that brings with it the burden of a troubling trial of affliction, will also inevitably and eventually increase our gracing and gifting as believers. To really know that brings great peace and fearlessness into our hearts as God's children. The uglier and more painful the experience, the greater and more powerful the received grace in our lives will be.

That means, in our lives, there are no wasted tears or trials, no purposeless pain or suffering, no meaningless affliction or trouble. It's hard to believe that when we endure trials. It is sometimes impossible to reason or even imagine how such a trial could actually benefit us. But beyond human reason and understanding are the purpose and grace of God for our lives. The misery or our today becomes valuable and meaningful when God's grace turns it into a ministry to others in our tomorrow. The trials and tribulations of our life today are helping equip us for the triumphs and testimonies of our tomorrow.

God has allowed the scars of His son to remain visible for all eternity as a continuous reminder of the great cost and priceless value of our salvation. The suffering of Christ has great meaning and power today and forever. The scars He bears are beautiful because of what they mean to God and to mankind. The scars you bear are also beautiful for what they mean to God, to you and to others.

I like to tell pastors that I don't trust any minister who doesn't have a limp. Of course that reference has nothing to do with man or woman's physical condition, instead it is a reference to Jacob. Jacob wrestles with an angel until the angel gave him God's blessing, which included a new name, Israel. Jacob refused to let the angel go until he was blessed, so the angel smote Jacob's hip and semi-crippled him. He could still walk and function but he did so with an obvious and visible limp.

It may seem unfair to be both blessed and crippled by God at the same time, however I don't think Jacob would have given up his blessing to get rid of his limp. I think he happily limped along the rest of his life being reminded with every step both of the price he paid and the promise he received on the day of his blessing. As others quickly learned of his amazing encounter with God, his limp represented to them a man who had touched God and been transformed by the touch of God.

The limp we have as leaders and believers is a reminder and symbol of our humanity and of a turning point in life where we met God. Something that has changed us because we allowed it to. Something that has scarred or marked us. Our limp or scar may look like a weakness or infirmity to others, but we know it is really a reminder of our strength in God's grace.

CHAPTER 18

Don't Give Up! Give God the chance to write a good ending to your story.

My wife lovingly calls me Lazarus. You know, just like the biblical character Jesus raised back to life after he'd been dead four days. She and I both know, probably more than anyone else, that what God has done in resurrecting and restoring our lives is truly a miraculous thing. Like the story of Lazarus, almost everyone who knew us or was familiar with our story came to the same conclusion that our situation was so hopeless that, especially in this city, we had a zero chance of having any kind of future here. But, they were all wrong. They were wrong because, in their evaluations and conclusions about our lives and futures, they simply didn't consider the most important factor that makes any comeback possible- God.

I've written this book and told my story so that you might have hope for a comeback in your life. Please know this my friend, no one is rooting for your comeback more than our loving God! In the story of your life, don't stay stuck in the chapters dominated by loss and pain. Give God the chance to write a good ending to your story!

In my story, I confess I've done a thousand things wrong, but the one thing I did right was I didn't give up. That's really all God needs to start and complete a comeback in your story. He is looking to see that you don't give up.

I discovered that my greatest enemy, the one that worked so tirelessly to detour, deceive, and defeat me, was discouragement. I discovered that discouragement is always the greatest when breakthrough is the closest. Never make an important decision when you're discouraged. Discouragement is a reality in life, and we all know what it feels like to be discouraged; but so much of what God can do in giving your life a great comeback is entirely dependent on your ability to overcome discouragement first. People that quit, that don't engage their faith in the promises of God for a breakthrough and comeback, always limit the extent of God's activity in their lives. The God of the comeback, who passionately and unconditionally loves you, who desperately longs for your healing and restoration, can only unleash the full force of His abilities into your life with your full permission and cooperation.

God has created you to be a dream machine. I call the sanctuary of our church the Dream Room. It is there, when God's children powerfully experience His presence and word, that I witness the remarkable moments in people's lives when their hearts begin to dream again.

Your heart was made to dream.

You know your heart is healthy when you begin to dream again! God gives our comeback to us in a dream before He makes it a reality. If our hearts can dream it, God can do it! Discouragement keeps our hearts dreamless, and that's why we must wage war against the presence of discouragement in our lives.

Discouragement blinds us to the heavenly vision and purpose God always has for us, and is getting ready to show us.

Discouragement keeps our mind and emotions tied to the failures, disappointments, and heartaches of our past. Hope is oxygen to our souls. When we are deprived of it our souls suffocate. Discouragement and hope are mortal enemies that wage an unceasing battle in our hearts for supremacy. Whichever one we focus on and feed the most becomes strengthened to overpower the other.

The promises of God's word are fuel and food for our heart's hope and faith. Time spent in prayer and worship builds up our immunity against the disease of discouragement. Hope is the normal atmosphere in the Kingdom of God. Hope is the greenhouse where the seeds of God's word and the dream of our hearts flourish and grow. Discouragement is a dry and barren desert where the only things that thrive are unwanted weeds. Because I was discouraged so intensely and for so long, it eventually opened the door and let its big brother, depression, come into my life. Now, I recognize that the longer I experience and tolerate the presence of discouragement, the more vulnerable I become to discouragement on steroids, which is depression.

At one point in my life, I became so discouraged that I wrote an entire country music album. The amusing thing was that I had never liked or even listened to country music. I tell people, jokingly of course, that at the very bottom of the valley of discouragement, they're playing country music! All joking aside, I believe in the power of music. I think—I know—that it's important to surround your soul with worship and praise music, especially when you're feeling tired and discouraged. The Lord gave me the gift of playing piano as an 18 year-old college student, and almost everyday since then, I have worshipped the Lord on my piano. My children all grew up hearing their father, often late at night, play spontaneous songs of worship to God on our piano. I speak from first hand experience:

> Worship heals.
> Worship changes the atmosphere.
> Worship changes the outcome.
> Worship gives us things we don't deserve to have and takes us places we don't deserve to be.

Our church has always been known as a place of intense worship. Why? Because its pastor is a passionate worshipper of Jesus. Here's a secret I wish I could spread throughout the body of Christ: worshipping pastors produce worshipping churches. I can't imagine living this life without having the glorious and life-changing encounters that worshipping God has brought me. Before I was a pastor or leader, I was a worshipper. When I'm no longer a pastor to people, I'll still be a worshipper to God. Worship will be our eternal identity and activity in heaven.

> Your story is not over.
> God's not done.
> The best chapters of your life are yet to come.
> Forgive the people that have hurt you, and God will anoint you to forget the pain they've caused you.
> Keep exposing your heart to God's love and word until it starts to dream again.
> Believe that you are who God says you are in His word.

Believe that God can do for you what He says He can do for you in His word.

Refuse to tolerate the presence and control of discouragement in your life.

Fortify the presence of your God-given hope by feeding it God's word, and by letting the Holy Spirit speak to you through visions, dreams and prophecy.

Recognize and resist the enemy's attempts to cover you in shame and condemnation. Condemnation is never from God, and the Bible says in Romans 8:1, "There is therefore now NO CONDEMNATION to those who are in Christ Jesus..."

Keep renewing your mind with God's word until you're completely convinced that God has a COMEBACK in any and every area of your life where you've experienced a setback.

It's always a SETUP when a crowd has gathered to watch your SETBACK. Why? Because they're also about to witness your supernatural COMEBACK!

Don't let your treasure be found in the value you have for what people think about you (reputation), but make it your greatest aim to live for an audience of One- your loving God (integrity).

I pray in the mighty name of Jesus Christ that the same God who supernaturally resurrected and restored my life, does the same and even more for you. I pray that you would know and experience the greatness and glory of the God of the Comeback. Amen. God bless you, my friend.

ABOUT THE AUTHOR

In God of the Comeback Dr. Maiden reminds us that God's plans and purposes are never undone by situations that arise. Through his own personal story Dr. Maiden will encourage you to trust in the God who will bring you through the storms into your destiny.